DAY TRADING FROM ZERO

A BEGINNER'S STEP-BY-STEP GUIDE TO AVOID TRAGIC MISTAKES AND GET OFF TO A GOOD START IN DAY TRADING USING THE BEST SKILLS AND STRATEGIES AVAILABLE

By

Andrew Pemberton

Table of Contents

Introduction

Traditionally, most of the people who used to trade in the stock market were those who work in brokerages, trading houses, and financial institutions. Thanks to the influx of technology and the internet, there has been a rise in online trading places. Brokers have taken advantage of that, and individuals can play the games online. This has turned out to be a growing and lucrative business. The secret is to make sure that you completely understand what it entails, practice, and learn more. For the newbies, it can be a little bit challenging. You do not need to worry since, with the right strategy, approach, and plan, you are bound to succeed. What you should know is that even the most experienced day traders have their failures and a bad day. First, you need to know how day trading works.

How Does Day Trading Work?

What you should know is that day trading is not an investment. It involves purchasing an asset stake, hopefully, to make a profit over a set period. The length of time to anticipate the profit is subjective. This because most investors are always open to the idea of holding their assets for many years, which can end up to decades. The secret is to be aware of the industry you are investing in. Always look for firms that are known to make great profit margins. They are the best since your profitability, and great returns are guaranteed. Look for debt-free firms, have a strong product line, and do not have any pending lawsuits.

Day traders will buy and sell financial securities within a day. Traders will look for different sources of funds to buy the securities. Most of them will borrow funds and buy when the security prices are lower, anticipating them to rise later in the day. The basic principle is always to buy when the cost is low and sell when it is high. That is where you will get the best profit margins. This s always managed at a compressed time limit.

An example is when a trader buys around 500 shares at 9:00 am. After 30 minutes, the price goes up, and he decides to sell. He will end up making a profit for that day less the commission chargeable and any applicable taxes. You need to know that when you sell a stock or investment that you have owned for less than a year. It is normally taxed against your gains. They are taxed at 35% as opposed to the long-term ones that are taxed at around 20%. It is evident that when day trading, you should put into consideration the taxation concept.

The profit margin will increase based on the number of trades. Day traders always limit their risks by not owning their stock overnight to avoid drastic price changes. The main reason could be market volatility hence the need for immediate response. Day traders will act quickly and make fast decisions, unlike other traders who will take time to make any decision.

What Does a Day Trader Do?

Day trader's typical day involves participating in financial markets purchasing and disposing of stocks, forex, and other securities. Their work also involves closing positions to make small and regular profits. There are different types of traders—the small-scale ones, the independent ones with their home space, and the ones based in institutions. Apart from trading, they also manage and maintain different markets and do research. They also do an analysis of financial notes based on securities and exchange information with the other traders.

This type of trading is considered to be on the fast lane and requires someone who can handle a lot of challenges and stress. You will need a deep and clear understanding of how the market works. You will also need to possess the required trading skills to be successful. One of the skills includes the ability to analyze different price charts.

A day trader always starts its day before the financial markets open. They will check all the financial information to help in economic development, analytical reports, market data, and any political news. They also check and analyze the technical indicators and any results from the trading. The information they rely upon is from their subscription and analyst. This information is crucial and helps in decision-making.

The other duty for a day trader is to check any confirmation from trading. The confirmation is from the trading from the previous day. Then they check any activity notes and the overnight position that they hold. In case there are any errors, they need to be fixed immediately since all the charges are billed to the trader.

Then they will ensure that the trades have been successfully settled. The next thing will be to check the cash that they got and the profit in their trading account. What they confirm is if there is a purchase that was not sent to their accounts. Or a third party to a sale that has not paid for the security. They need to immediately address that since it is bound to affect their trading ability.

The most important part of a trader's life is when the market opens. The trader will put all the orders in the open that is entirely dependent on their style and plans. Then they will enter follow-ups on the trades that they intend to sell or buy.

They spend most of the day doing analysis and analyzing financial reports and charts with price movements. An hour before the market closes, the trader will then close all the positions before leaving for the day. This is to ensure that there are no overnight risks.

Making a profit is any trader's goal. When they are private traders, they will bank all the profit. For the employed ones, they earn a percentage of the gains since they trade under customers' accounts. When there is a loss, nothing is paid. They need to refund the cash advances to the trading account.

Other duties of a day trader include doing market analysis and observation of trading strategies formulation and completing a trade with brokers. They ensure that they sell all assets by the close of the day and have the investment as cash and profits. They also cut losses when there is a failure in investment. They are required to complete tax returns and do transaction recording.

Techniques Used in Day Trading

You need to have the best techniques when it comes to trading. Day trading can be considered simple or complicated, based on the techniques and approaches that you use. The best techniques are the ones that will help in maximizing profit and minimize price movements. To have effective approaches, you will need to depend on in-depth analysis, use price charts, and price indicators. The patterns will help in predicting price changes in the future.

We will illustrate the best strategies and techniques to adopt that will help all traders on a different level, from beginners to experts. You will be able to know how to position yourself and know about useful resources. The important thing to note is ensuring that you pick a technique that will perfectly fit with your preference, requirements, and style.

When you are starting in the world of trading, do not be in a hurry to master all the technical terms and processes. Starts with the basics first; do not think that having a complicated technique is what will make you successful. You should know that the simpler your plan is, the more effective it will be.

You need to understand all the components of money management. You need to know the amount of money you are ready to risk as your capital. Note that it is not advisable to put down anything above 2% of your capital for each trade. Ensure that you are aware that you are also bound to make losses.

Ensure you know how to manage your time. Day trading will need you to input a lot of your time. And you should also know how to strike a balance between your professional and personal life. Do not expect to allocate like an hour or two, and expect to have great returns. Be attentive in monitoring the financial markets and looking for new trading chances.

Start small; do not be in a hurry to invest a lot of capital. Learn a lot, master the skill then invest more. You can start with at least three stocks daily. It is considered wise to start with fewer stocks and make great returns that investing in more and not gaining anything.

The only way to understand the market and master it is by learning a lot. You need to keep yourself informed on what is happening. Be updated on what is happening, any news, or occasions. Ensure you know about asset implications, especially when there is a shift in economic policies.

Be consistent with your trading. Deliver work with the same morale and spirit. Depend on logical facts and a strategic plan. Always ensure that your timing is always right. This is because when the market opens, it becomes volatile. Experts will be able to read the patterns, and you should be able to bide the time. You can hold on in the first minutes of trading. There are several components that each trader is s meant to know. Be it a beginner or experienced, you should master the components.

Volatility

This component will illustrate the potential gain in each trade. Great volatility means greater gains or losses.

Liquidity

This component makes a trader enter and exit the trading period and still manage a stable and attractive price.

Volume

Volume is a component that will indicate the number of times a stock has been traded over a certain time. It is commonly known as the average daily trading volume. When the volume is high, it indicates higher gains or interest in the trade. When the volume increases, it means that there is a change in price.

What Is the Market to Day Trade?

There are three different markets for day trading: forex, futures, and the stock market. Most people are aware of the stock market and not of futures and forex.

Stock Market

When people think of day trading, stock market comes into their mind first. It is considered the best when it comes to buying and selling company shares. And you'll need to exit all positions by the close of the trading period. There is a requirement to hold at least $25k in your account; anything less will not be accepted in day trading. The required capital to start is $30k.

Future Market

This is another market for day trading, where there is an agreement between a seller and a buyer. They agree to sell or buy at an agreed amount at a certain time. Traders make their gains from price fluctuations. This is from the difference computed between what is bought or sold and when the position closes. For this market, you do not need too much capital, a minimum of $3500, and a maximum of $5k is enough to start.

Chapter 1. Tools and Platforms Use to Trade

Trading Platform

Online trading programs are often provided by agents either at no cost or a discount fee in exchange for keeping a funded account or making a predetermined variety of transactions each month. The finest trading platforms provide a mixture of powerful features and reduced prices.

Key Takeaways

Trading programs are software tools used to handle and implement market rankings. Platforms vary from first-order entry displays for novice investors to complicated and complex toolkits with live streaming quotes and charts for advanced traders. Traders and traders must take numerous factors into account and equilibrium trade-offs when choosing a trading platform.

Principles of Trading Platform

A trading platform is an application That Permits traders and investors to place transactions and track accounts through fiscal intermediaries. Platforms might also be specially tailored to certain markets, like stocks, monies, alternatives, or futures markets.

As their title suggests, commercial systems have been aimed at day traders and retail investors. They're characterized by ease-of-use along with also a range of useful features, such as news feeds and graphs, for investor education and study.

Dealers use an assortment of different trading platforms based on their trading design and quantity.

Selecting a Platform

When picking between trading platforms, both investors and traders should consider both the charges involved and the attributes available. Day dealers, along with other short-term traders, might need attributes like grade two quotations and market manufacturer depth charts to help out with decision-making. On the other hand, choices traders might need tools that are particularly designed to picture options plans.

Fees are another significant consideration when picking trading platforms. By way of instance, traders that use scalping for a trading approach may gravitate towards platforms using reduced prices. Generally, lower prices are almost always preferable, but there might be trade-offs to take into account. By way of instance, low prices might not be valuable if they interpret to fewer attributes and informational study.

Some trading platforms can be reverted to a particular intermediary or even agent, though other trading platforms are only accessible when working with a specific broker or agent. Because of this, investors should also consider the standing of the intermediary or agent before committing to a certain trading platform to implement trades and handle their accounts.

Ultimately, trading platforms might have particular requirements to be eligible due to their usage. By way of instance, day trading platforms might require that dealers have $25,000 at equity inside their account and be qualified for margin trading. In contrast, alternatives platforms might require approval to exchange a variety of kinds of choices before having the ability to utilize the trading platform.

Popular Trading Platforms

There are hundreds--or even thousands--of different trading platforms, including those four popular choices:

Interactive Agents

Interactive Brokers is the most popular trading platform for professionals using reduced fees and access to markets across the world.

Trade Station

Trade Station is a favorite trading platform for algorithmic dealers who prefer to perform trading strategies utilizing automated scripts developed with easy language.

Robinhood

It started as a portable program and today has a web interface too. The platform makes cash from many sources, from interest on money in its account to promoting order flow to big brokerages.

The very popular platform for all foreign exchange (forex) Marketplace participants is MetaTrader that will be a trading platform that interfaces with several distinct brokers. Its MQL scripting language is now a favorite tool for those seeking to automate trading in monies.

Selecting the Proper Day-Trading Software

Computer software has made it Simple to automate trading, particularly for short term intensive tasks like day trading, making the use of trading programs popular.

The discussion continues within the profit potential, which will be realistically derived from day-trading actions utilizing online trading platforms, as broker fees and commissions are believed to eliminate the significant part of available gain possible. It thus becomes extremely important to choose the ideal day-trading software using a cost-benefit analysis, evaluation of its applicability to individual trading requirements and strategies, in addition to the features and functions you want.

Day trading is a currency trading action at which purchase or market positions are accepted and closed on precisely the same trading day to earn gains in smaller price differentials on large purchase volumes by regular buying and selling, typically on leverage.

Key Takeaways

Day trading applications demand tools and order entry systems that permit day traders to perform their job in an efficient and consistent method. These programs frequently feature automated trading based on parameters determined by the day dealer, allowing for orders to be routed to the marketplace faster than individual reflexes. Selecting the most appropriate day trading software program necessitates knowing the costs and advantages of every offering for you to optimize its performance.

What's Day-Trading Software?

Day-trading software comprises a computer program, generally supplied by brokerage companies, to assist customers in executing their day-trading actions in an efficient and timely way. They frequently automate analysis and input transactions on their own that allow traders to reap gains that would be tough to attain by mere mortals. By way of instance, a day dealer might find it impossible to manually monitor two technical indicators (such as 50- and 200-day moving averages) on three distinct shares of her or his choice.

Still, an automatic day-trading software can certainly take action and put trades after the set standards are satisfied.

The characteristics and functions available can vary from 1 software package to another and can arrive in various versions. Aside from agents, independent sellers also give day-trading applications, which often have more advanced capabilities.

How Can Day-Trading Software Work?

Analytical instruments keep the assessment of Current holdings (if any), marketplace developments, and attributes to accordingly behave on these. Any day-trading applications will demand a one-time installment of trading strategy together with establishing the trading limitations; setting the machine on vital information and allowing it to execute the transactions.

An example: Assume stock ABC is dual-listed on either the New York Stock Exchange (NYSE) or NASDAQ. You're searching for arbitrage chances, and there's day-trading software available to this, so, you prepare the following:

Select Inventory ABC for Arbitrage and Choose Two Markets (NYSE and NASDAQ) for Trading

Assuming both thighs of intraday exchange prices you a total of $0.10 per share for commission and brokerage, you plan to search for cost differentials between the two markets over that sum. So that you place (state $0.20 or over) as the cost differential--i.e., the program must execute a simultaneous purchase and sell purchase just when the bidding and ask prices on the two markets are different by $0.20 (or much more).

Establish the Number of Stocks to Be Purchased and Sold in 1 Sequence (say 10,000 stocks) and Permit this Installment to Go Live

Say the Program explains that ABC has estimates of $62.10 on NYSE and $62.35 on Nasdaq (a differential of $0.25) for orders of over the established limit of 10,000 shares. The day-trading applications will commence trade as it fulfills with the specified standards, and will send orders into the two trades (purchase at reduced priced and market at even higher priced). If everything goes well, this day-trading applications will create ((62.35 -- 62.10) -- 0.10 = 0.15) * (10,000) = $1,500 of net gain for your dealer super-fast.

Further improvements in the applications above may include stop-loss attributes --state if just your purchase trade gets implemented but not the market. How should the day-trading applications proceed using the long-standing? A few options can be contained as improved features in the program:

Proceed to Search for Market Chances at Identified Costs for a Particular Moment

If no opportunities are recognized in the designated period, square off the place at a reduction. Change into an averaging strategy --purchase more shares at lower costs to decrease the overall cost.

Features and Functionality

A good deal of these kinds of day-trading actions can be installed via day-trading applications, and so it's extremely important to pick the perfect one fitting your requirements. Some features of great day-trading applications:

- Platform freedom: Unless A dealer is operating exceptionally intricate calculations for Day-trading requiring high-end computers that are dedicated, it's sensible to go using an online program offering. Benefits include connectivity from anyplace, no manual installments of updates, and no maintenance prices. But if you're using highly sophisticated algorithms that need sophisticated computing, then it's far better to consider committed computer-based installable applications, even though that will be pricey.

- Your particular needs daily trading: Are you currently observing a straightforward day-trading approach of moving-average monitoring on Stocks, or are you seeking to implement an intricate delta-neutral trading strategy including stocks and options? Do you require a currency feed, or are you currently trading on specific products such as binary choices? Trusting the promises on stockbrokers' site content isn't enough to know the offering. Request a trial version also completely evaluate it during the first phase. Alternately, check the screen-by-screen tutorial (if available) in the stockbroker or seller to know the ideal match for the day-trading needs.

- Added Attributes: Day trading efforts to capitalize on short-term price movements over the day. Such short term price movements are subsequently driven primarily by information and distribution and need (among other variables). Does your day-trading strategy demand information, graphs, Grade two info, exclusive connectivity into specific markets (such as OTC), personal data feeds, etc.)? If so, are those contained in the applications, or would the dealer need to subscribe to them individually from different resources, hence raising the price?

Analytical Features

Pay attention to this record of analytical features it provides. Listed below are a couple of these:

- Technical Indicators/Pattern Recognition: For dealers who try to gain from calling the upcoming cost level and management, a wealth of technical indicators can be obtained. When the dealer finalizes the specialized indicators to follow along, they ought to guarantee that the day-trading program affirms the essential automation for efficient processing of transactions based on the desirable technical index.

- Arbitrage Opportunities Recognition: To profit from the small cost difference of a dual-listed discuss on multiple niches, allows profit opportunities, and can be among those typically followed approaches employing day-trading software. It needs a link to both markets, the capacity to inspect cost differences as they happen, and implement trades in a timely way.

- A mathematical model-based approach: Few automated trading approaches based on mathematical models exist--such as the delta-neutral trading system --which enables trading on a mixture of choices. Its inherent security, where transactions are put to cancel negative and positive deltas, proves that the portfolio delta is preserved at zero. The day-trading software ought to have the in-built intellect to estimate the recent holdings, confirm available market costs, and implement trades for both equity and alternatives as required.

- Trend following approaches: Another massive collection of approaches commonly implemented via day-trading software.

Chapter 2. How to Find Profitable Stocks to Trade

Some of your family members love this idea and decide they will stick with you. Your sister does not, she sells her stock, and now that share of the profits is yours again. Instead of just holding on to it, you decide to "go public" with your stock. You split this⅕ share into ten smaller shares and then go to the town meeting with your new public stock. In your particular town, this is very normal, and lots of other people there have public shares of their stocks. Billy's Car Washing Company, Linda's Dog Walker, Susie's Lawn Mowers are all represented. There, neighbors can invest in all the kids' companies. You announce the value of your stock, and your neighbors can decide if they want to buy some.

Now, if we take this example, turn weeks into years, and increase the dollar figures exponentially, we have the basic structure of the stock market. There are some other key players we need to factor in, though.

First off, each company is not owned and run by one person. Instead, there is a board that votes on big decisions like what should be done with the profits, and therefore with the stocks. Let us take a look at another fictional company to see what role the board plays.

Popper's Pinatas Inc

$40 per share

20,000 shares outstanding

Market Capitalization: $800,000 $40 x 20,000 shares

This company made $100,000 in profits this year.

When this $100,000 is divided among shareholders, it yields a profit of $5 for each share.

Another player in the real stock market that was missing from our lemonade stand example is the stockbroker. If you imagine the whole town in the meeting above, each one is shouting and jockeying for the stocks they want you can see how little would get done.

The actual marketplace is much, much bigger, so we rely on brokers to do the buying and selling. These are representatives of shareholders who make a list of intentions, called orders, into the market, and fill them on behalf of the customer.

The list of possible investments is enough to make your head spin, but it is important to remember that these strategies are nothing more than tools. Think about it this way: a hammer is a great tool for driving a nail, but it is hopelessly ineffective if you are trying to scramble an egg. Keep in mind your ultimate investment goals, and you will be able to choose the appropriate instrument to meet those goals.

Investment Options

Savings Accounts

This is a type of investment that you are no doubt familiar with but may not think of as an investment. The probable reason for that is that the rate of return is comparably low. While savings accounts provide quite a lot of security, given that they are protected up to $250,000 by the FDIC, the interest rate is low. Looking at several leading banks show returns well under 1% for their highest yielding savings accounts. The upside of this type of investment is that you can deposit or withdraw as you like, at whatever time suits you.

Certificates of Deposit

In return for this guarantee, the bank agrees to pay an interest rate over the lifetime of the agreement. It is called the maturity of the CD.

CDs offer benefits such as the certainty of a return due to interest and protection from inflation. During periods of high inflation, locking your money up in a CD ensures that you will get that amount out when it reaches maturity, whatever has gone on in the economy during that time. It also ensures that you will get whatever return was guaranteed when it was issued.

The downsides, though, are significant. If you need to cash a CD out before it matures, you will pay a hefty fee, often totaling the full amount of interest that has been paid on it at that point. This fact means that buying a CD limits your ability to capitalize on higher interest rates that may be offered down the road. If you buy a CD with a 3% interest rate and then see another one offered with a 5% return, you will not be able to roll it into the more profitable rate without paying those fees.

Money Market Accounts

A Money Market Account MMA can be thought of as a blend of a traditional savings account and a CD. They usually require a minimum balance to be maintained, offer a higher interest rate than a savings account, and allow a limited number of transactions usually six per year. Like savings accounts, they are insured by the FDIC, limiting the risk associated.

Be careful not to confuse bank MMAs with investment accounts of the same name. From an investment house, this refers to short-term investments in mutual funds that come with no guaranteed return and are not FDIC insured.

Stocks

Stocks are investments in equity. They are tied to the success of a particular company and can be thought of as part-ownerships. This type of investment does not come with the protection of federal insurance, so you will need to protect your money in other ways. Diversification comes into play here, but another important aspect of that protection is carefully examining prospective companies before investing.

Mutual Funds

A mutual fund is a group of investments managed by a professional money manager. Depending on which fund you are looking at, you may find them made up of high-dividend stocks, blue-chip or so-called "bellwether" stocks, foreign stocks, or a mix of those and others. Unlike individual stocks, mutual funds are valued and traded only once per day. Because so many people are sharing the reward and the risk, mutual funds confer less risk on each investor, but also a lower chance of yielding a high return.

Also, most funds require a fee to be paid to the company issuing and managing them. Conventional wisdom predicts that a higher fee would correlate with a higher rate of return, but this does not bear out. Historically, mutual funds charging higher fees net lower returns for their investors, so make sure to do your homework about the individual funds' management and historical return.

Exchange-Traded Funds

Many people do not know the difference between an Exchange Traded Fund ETF and a mutual fund. While both are comprised of stocks chosen by a money manager, an ETF tends to focus in one area agriculture, foreign markets, real estate, etc. and many tie their composition to the overall composition of the S&P 500. Another key difference is that ETFs can be traded at any point during the trading day, not just at the closing. While this offers an ability to pivot more quickly, there are usually fees associated with each trade, so only large transactions make sense here to minimize the ratio of the fee to the trade.

Some ETFs even offer leverage, which is the ability to borrow money to purchase stock. This can increase the ability to seize opportunities where a boom is expected, but it is a double-edged sword. If the expectations fail to materialize, that debt is a liability.

Bonds

A bond is, at its root, a loan. The purchaser loans a certain amount to a company and is guaranteed a certain interest rate every year for the life of the bond. This interest is called the "coupon rate." The bond is issued with a set lifespan, at the end of which it reaches its "maturity date." If a 30-year bond were purchased for $100 with a coupon rate of 5%, the purchaser would receive $5 each year for 30 years, and then get their original $100 back.

Three Types of Bonds

Treasury Bonds- these are issued by the United States Treasury, and as you might expect, with the Federal Government behind them, they carry very little risk. Naturally, they also have very low-interest rates.

Corporate Bonds- these are bonds issued by companies and are as reliable as the company itself.

Municipal Bonds- Municipal bonds are issued by a state, city, or other local governments. Depending on your residency, investing in these bonds may come with tax incentives. Be aware, though, that just because these are investments in governments, they are not always secure. Governments are vulnerable to instabilities that can overwhelm them, taking your investment down on the way.

Foreign Currency and Stocks

Trading in foreign stocks is one of the riskiest and exciting aspects of investing. Not only are you placing a wager on the company you are investing in, but you are also betting that the exchange rate between your money and the currency you are investing in will remain favorable. While this is a thrilling and potentially highly lucrative area of investing, you should attain a strong knowledge of investing strategies and global macroeconomics beforehand.

Real Estate

Real estate investment is not limited to buying homes or commercial buildings. There are real estate focused mutual funds, real estate investment trusts which invest in rental properties, mortgage-backed securities, and mortgage-backed obligations. When the real estate market is strong, these can be quite secure and profitable. As we saw through after 2008, there is no guarantee that it will remain strong and can become a liability in down markets.

In most types of investment, the decisions are made for you by people who may or may not have an expertise that you trust. When you buy your stocks, you bring to the transaction personal knowledge, beliefs, and motivations. Stocks allow you to customize your portfolio to represent what you want your money to do for you and in the world.

Chapter 3. Candlesticks

Day trading is difficult, and if you do not take the time to pick a good strategy and learn it fully, it will become harder. The first strategy that we will take a look at is the candlestick strategy. There are a few options that come with it, and it often depends on which direction you think the market will go.

You can choose what time frame is used, but make sure that it is consistent with your whole chart. Some people go for the whole day, or you can choose an hour to help you out. The hollow or filled part of the chart will be the body, while the thin lines that show up below and above the body will be the high and low ranges, and they are known as the shadows (or you can call them the tails or the wicks).

One thing to remember here is that the hollow candlesticks that have a close that is greater than the open will indicate that there is some buying pressure. However, if there is a filled candlestick where the close comes out as less than the open will indicate that there is some selling pressure.

Bullish Engulfing Pattern

Bullish Candlesticks Example

As mentioned, there are a few different types of candlesticks that you can work with, and the first option will be the bullish candlesticks. Candles that have a larger body towards the top are considered bullish, and they mean that the buyers will be the ones who are in control of the price. When you see this kind of chart, realize that it is likely that the buyers will keep pushing so that the price goes higher. This kind of candlestick is not only going to tell you the price, but it is also able to tell you that the bulls are winning and that they have the power.

Bearish Candlesticks Example

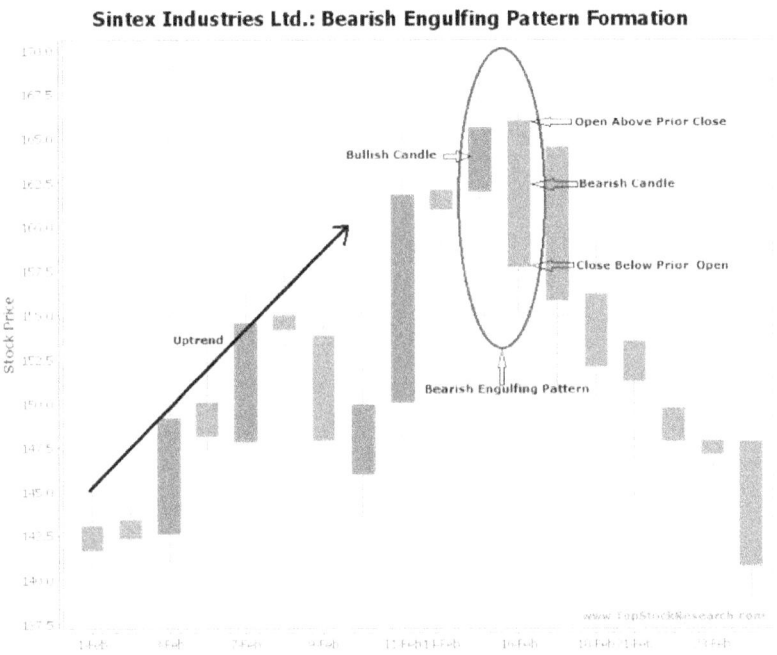

Sintex Industries Ltd.: Bearish Engulfing Pattern Formation

There are also bearish candles. They will work a bit differently than you will find with the bullish candlesticks and can have you react differently. When you see a bearish candle, it means that the sellers are the ones in control of the price action that goes on in the market and that buying would probably not be a good idea at this time.

When you see a candle that is filled and has a pretty long filled body, it means that your opening was high, but the closing was low. It is one way to tell that the market is bearish right now, and it is probably not a good idea to get into the market at this time. You will probably not get a good price for the stocks because the market price is going down, and there are not as many buyers interested right now.

Just by being able to read these candlesticks, you will be able to generate an opinion for how the stock will generally, or the price action. You need to understand which party (the buyer or the seller) is in charge of the price can help you determine whether now is a good time to purchase the stock or not. When you have a bullish market, the price will keep going up, so it is a good idea to jump in and then sell the stock at a higher price. But if you are in a bearish market, the price is most likely going to go down, and it is not in your best interest to make a purchase.

Indecision Candlesticks

Some candlesticks are known as indecision candlesticks. There are two main types of indecision candlesticks, including spinning tops and Dojis.

Spinning Tops Example

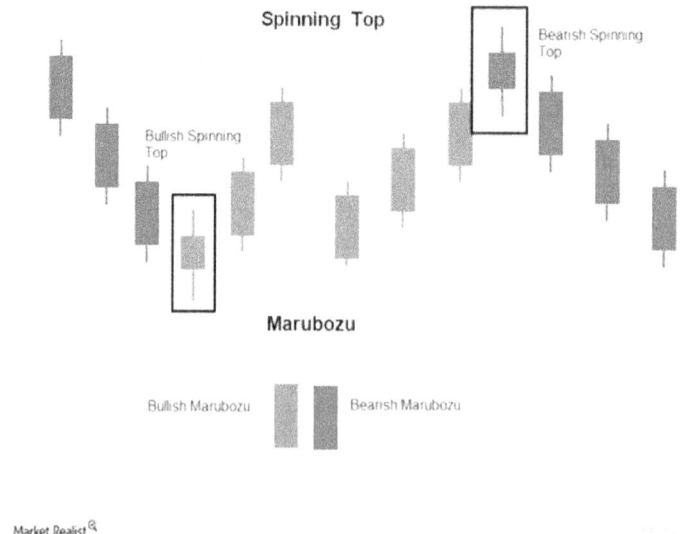

32

The spinning tops are candles that have the high wicks that are similarly sized and then low wicks that happen to be larger than the bottom and look a bit indecisive. With these candlesticks, the sellers and the buyers have powers that are pretty close to even. No one is really in control over the price of the stock, but there is still a fight that is going on. The volume on these will be lower because the traders want to wait and see whether the buyers or the sellers will be the ones that wend.

You will notice that a trend in the price is often going to change right away after this kind of indecision candle, once the fight has been won by either the sellers or the buyers, so it is worth your time to recognize this kind of price action. Sometimes it will go well, and the price will go up, but the market could also go the other way, and you could see the price drop.

Dojis

Another type of candlestick pattern that you should watch out for is the Doji. There are a few forms and shapes of this, but they are either going to have no body to the candlestick or at least a really small body. When you see that there is a Doji in the chart, it means that there is a fight between the bulls and the bears, and no one is winning yet.

There are some times when the Doji will have a bottom and top wick that are unequal. If the top of the wick ends up being longer, it means that the buyer tried to get the price higher, but they were unsuccessful. They may show that the buyers are starting to lose power, and the sellers may start to take over. On the other hand, if the bottom wick is longer, this means that the sellers tried to push the price down, and they were not successful. This may mean that there will be a takeover of the price action by the bulls.

You can use this to help you see what trends are going on. If one of these candlesticks shows up during a bullish trend, it means that the bulls are wearing out, and now the bears are trying to take over control of the price. If this candlestick forms when there is a bearish downward trend, it suggests that now the bears are tired and now the buyers or the bulls will take over the price. This can help you to see when a trend is about to occur in the market and can help you to make some smart decisions.

The candlestick pattern is a great way to predict how the market is going. When the market is going up based on these candlesticks, you will want to purchase and then sell before they go down. When the market is going down based on these candlesticks, you will either want to stay out of the market if you are not already in, or you will want to sell before the price goes down and you lose too much money. Take some time to learn how to make these charts, and you will find that they are a fantastic way for you to monitor the way that the market is going.

Chapter 4. Basic and Profitable Strategies

These strategies rely on patterns, indicators, and charts to forecast potential price movements. We will give you a complete breakdown of the strategies.

Breakout

This strategy is used to position a trader in the early stages of a trend, and it can cause volatility expansions, movement in price, and partial downside risk. A breakout is the movement of a stock price out of distinct support or the resistance level with a bigger volume. In situations where the price of the stock increases beyond the resistance, the trader gets into a long position and where it decreases lower than the support he gets into a short position. When the stock price increases above the price barrier, an increase in volatility is experienced, and stock prices follow the direction of the breakout. Breakouts are essential strategies because they mark the starting point of large price trends and swings as well as volatility increases in the future. These breakouts take place in all kinds of markets. The most volatile price movements are caused by breakouts of price patterns like flags or triangles and channel breakouts. It is well explained in our chart below; as volatility reduces during this period, it will usually increase after an increase in prices above the identified range.

Example of a Triangle Breakout

CLF Cleveland Cliffs Inc 119.46 -7.47 -5.89%
D: 11/15/2007 O:79.79 H:80.28 L:75.74 C:77.98 R:4.54 Y:116.4926

Breakout trading is a good strategy despite the timeframe. It doesn't matter whether you use charts or intraday the perceptions are universal. How do you find a good candidate?

It is important to think about and consider the stock's resistance levels and support in trading breakouts.

You should look at the number of times the stock has touched those parts; the more times they are touched, the more important and valid they become. At the same time, you should look at the period they have been in play; the longer the time, the better the results after a breakout.

Example of Numerous Reactions to Support over Time

You can see different patterns occurring as the prices are consolidating. You should always consider some formations when searching for a stock to trade. These formations are flags, channels, or triangles. Other than the patterns, you should also consider the length of time a stock has held on its resistance levels and consistency before choosing an excellent candidate to trade.

Scalping

It aims to take advantage of minute changes in price. A trader sells when the trade happens to be profitable. The risks are high, but it is an exciting and fast way to trade. The trader needs a high probability in trading to equate the risk to reward ratio. The trader looks out for attractive liquidity, volatile instruments, and the best time.

Scalping Example

Scalping can be implemented as a primary or supplementary style.

Primary Style

A scalper makes many trades in a day. He or she uses one-minute charts as the time frame is little, and the setups should be noticed as they form in the closest real-time possible. The trader can use some support systems like Level 2 quotations or Direct Access Trading. A direct-access broker is the best suited for this style as he or she can execute orders automatically.

Supplementary Style

This style is suitable for traders with extended time frames. The best way they utilize it is when the market is locked in a constricted range. In cases of longer time frames with no trends, choosing a shorter time frame discloses some exploitable trends that direct the trader to the scalp.

There is also another method called the "umbrella" concept that adds scalping to lengthy time frames. In this method, the trader maximizes profits by progressing his or her cost basis. Depending on a trade's setup, any system can be used for scalping. It makes scalping a risk management technique. In scalping, the risk/reward ratio of the profit should be close to 1:1. We can take a look at an example in trading if a trader positions himself for a scalp trade at $100 and the first stop at $99.90. With a simple calculation, we find the risk to be 10 cents. With that information, we should deduce that the risk/reward ratio of 1:1 will have arrived at $100.10.

Scalp trades can be carried out in both short and long sides. We can also use some traditional chart formation for scalpings such as triangles or cups and handles.

Momentum

A momentum strategy is suitable for beginners. It involves taking actions on new sources and spotting large trending moves supported by high volume. The opportunities are plenty, as you will always find a stock that is moving for 20-30% any day. If used correctly, this strategy is effective and quite simple. Nevertheless, you must make sure that you know the upcoming news and announcements on the earnings. If you trade well, you will notice a big difference in your daily profits even though you only need a few seconds on every trade.

Example of Momentum

Bull Flag Pattern

This pattern presents entries with low risks for strong stocks. They are easy to find but might give beginners a little difficulty in real-time. You should always look for patterns that support constant momentum. A trader can use scanners to find the patterns, but the addition of skills gives them a win.

Example of a Bull Flag Pattern

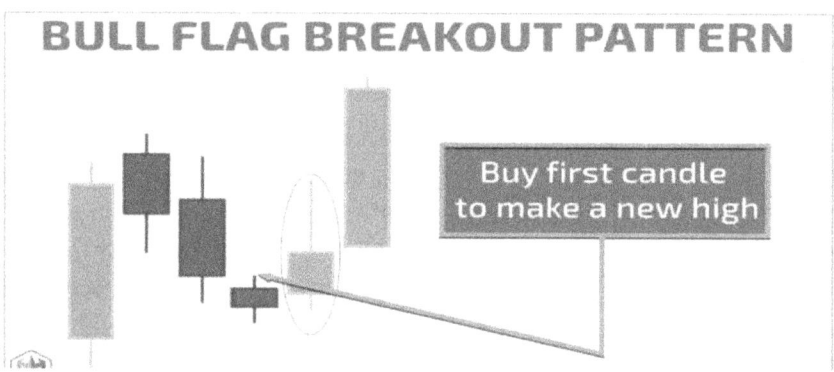

In this pattern, we should make an entry in the first candle to form a new high after a breakout. We then scan for stocks that have formed the big green candle of the Bull Flag. After doing that, we should wait for 2-3 candles to outline a pullback. Our entry is where the first green candle makes a new high green candle following the pullback. We can observe volume spikes exactly where the first candle makes a new high. These are traders positioning themselves and placing their buying orders.

We can look at a real-life example of a bull flag breakout. In the below picture, you can notice an opening drive on high volume followed by a consolidation on low volume that finally broke out. These are everyday patterns. All you need is knowledge of how to trade them.

A Real-Life Example of a Bull Flag Breakout

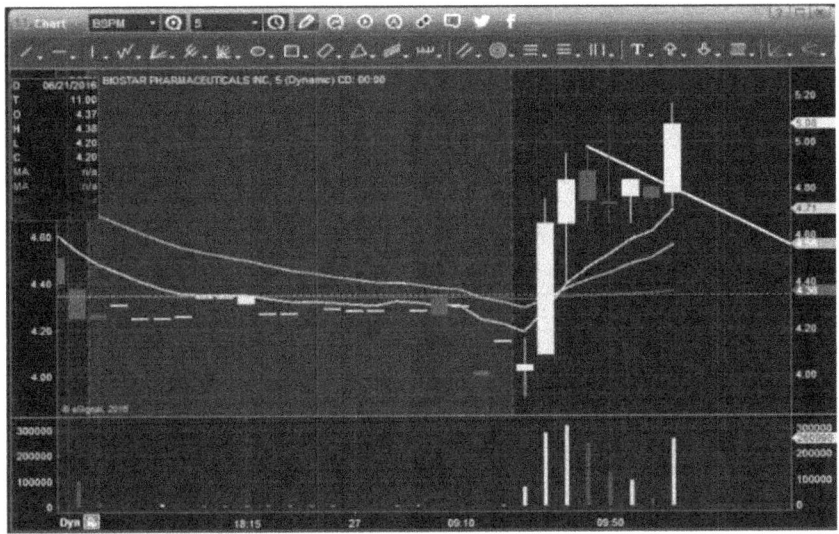

Flat Top Breakout

This pattern is similar to our previous pattern apart from the pullback. In the flat top break out, there is strong resistance on a flat top.

It is easily recognizable because of its flat top, and it happens on the formation of a few candles. This pattern is a result of big sellers hurdling at a certain price level. The prices can only move up if all the shares are bought.

In some cases, sellers put stop orders slightly above it, which can lead to an explosive breakout.

When buyers clear all the shares, the stop orders are triggered, making the stock price to shoot up. This action brings nice profits to traders.

Example of a Flat Top Breakout Pattern

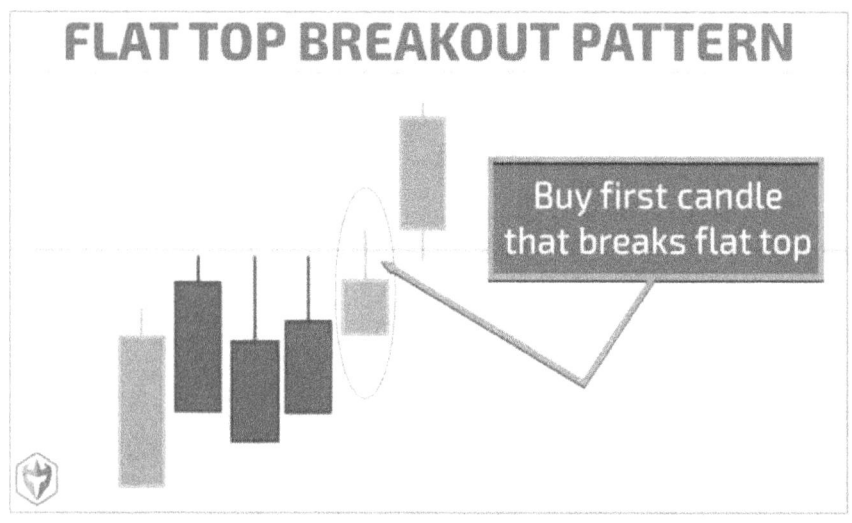

Reversal

A reversal is a price change towards an asset. It can happen to the downside or upside. A downside reversal follows an uptrend, while an upside reversal follows a downtrend. These reversals are founded on price direction and not on any periods on a chart. Some indicators like moving average can assist in identifying reversals and isolate separating trends. When a reversal happens, you cannot distinguish it from a pullback. For a successful differentiation, you should observe the behavior within a trend. A reversal continues and outlines a new trend, whereas a pullback halts, and the price moves back to the trend's direction.

They occur quickly and over days, weeks, and years. They occur in different time frames, and that makes it suitable for different traders. Reversals can be spotted using price actions and indicators. Sometimes the trend and reversal are spotted using moving averages. When the price is more than the moving average, the trend is usually up, and the price signals a possible price reversal drops lower than the moving average. We can also use trendlines to notice reversals. Seeing as an uptrend makes higher lows, we can draw a trendline to mark a trend reversal.

Reversals are not easy to spot as we need to distinguish them from brief pullbacks and noise.

Due to that reason, trading becomes a little difficult. False signs occur sometimes and confuse traders while other times, the reversals happen so fast, denying the traders a chance to avoid making losses.

The chart below indicates an uptrend making a move with a channel. It brings about higher lows and higher highs. The first break out of the price from the channel is at a point lower than the trendline. It shows a potential change in trend.

We can observe the price, making another lower low below the previous low in the channel. It signifies downside reversal.

The price keeps on reducing, making lower highs and lower lows. If the price can move above the downward trendline, this can signify a reversal.

Using reversals have its limitations, they are:

- It is difficult to tell whether they are reversals or pullbacks when they happen. This slight confusion may bring losses to traders as the price may have moved a considerable distance.
- There are many false signs in reversal.
- Ignoring a reversal brings trader losses.

Example of a Reversal in Play

Pivot Points

Using the pivot point strategy helps you to identify and act on dangerous resistance, support, or both.

It is mostly used in forex and to spot entry points by range-bound traders.

Also, it is used by breakout and trend traders to find key levels that should break so that a movie can be termed as a breakout. How do we calculate pivot points?

To calculate a pivot point, you should use the previous day's lows and highs in addition to a security's closing price.

The diagram below shows a step by step calculation of pivot point.

$P = (H - L - C) / 3$

In this formulae, P is the pivot point, H is high, L is the low and C is the closing price. After getting the pivot point, you will use it to calculate the resistance.

Resistance formulae:

1st Resistance $(R1) = (2*P) - L$
1st Support $(S1) = (2*p) - H$

Our next step is to calculate our second level of resistance and support as follows:

2nd Resistance $(R2) = P - (H - L)$
2nd Support $(S2) = P - (H - L)$

We then calculate our third level of resistance and support

3rd Resistance $= H - 2 * (P - L)$
3rd Support $= L - 2 * (H - P)$

*H stands for High
*P stands for pivot point calculated above
*L stands for Low
*R stands for Resistance
*S stands for Support

You should notice that all the formulas include our basic pivot point value. It is the reason why it is essential to come up with our pivot point level. The correct calculation of the basic pivot point value translates to correct subsequent calculations. If all the seven pivot points are added together, we come up with five lines on our chart, as shown below.

Example of Formation of Pivot Points When Added Together The

45

chart below is of two trading days.

The line separates the two days. Our first day helps us to determine the close, daily high, and daily low.

You are now looking at the chart below, which takes two trading days. The pink vertical lines separate each trading day.

We use the first trading session to attain the daily low, daily high, and close.

Our daily low is 14.28

Our daily high is 14.39

Our close is 14.37

We then use our formulas to determine our resistance, support, and pivot point.

Our next important issue to know about pivot points is how to interpret them. Pivot points can be used in two conducts.

The first conduct is to know the market trend. If it is broken in an ascending movement, it is a bullish market.

Chapter 5. Risk and the Account Management

There are three essential additives of day trading, which you need to master so that you can end up a hit on this enterprise: Sound Psychology, Effective Day Trading Strategies and Risk Management. These 3 are the pillars of day trading. If you are weak in a single area, the whole enterprise can collapse. It is a commonplace beginner's mistake to concentrate handiest on trading techniques. An effective strategy delivers an incredible expectancy as it produces better profits than losses over a specified period.

However, they ought to be nicely executed. Bear in thoughts that even the handiest method cannot assure fulfillment in every trade. No single method can assure you of by no means having a dropping trade or even experiencing a series of losses. This is the cause of danger control ought to be an essential part of each trading strategy.

The number one purpose new investors fail at day trading is their inability to manipulate dangers. We tend to accept revenue rapidly, and we additionally like to attend around until dropping trades return to even. By the time some novice investors discover ways to manipulate their dangers, their debts are depleted. To end up a hit in this craft, you must research danger control policies, and then nicely execute them.

There needs to be a clear rule that can guide you when you should get out of the exchange. It is k to commit errors for your trade. Even ultra-successful buyers nonetheless make bad selections despite their experience. You will lose lots of trades; however, don't forget to be a good loser. You want to take delivery of a loss. It is a critical part of day trading. As a beginner, you need to comply with the rules and plans of your trading method. And this is one of the challenges that you need to face on every occasion you are in an evil alternate.

Many amateur day buyers justify their decision to keep bad stocks by using saying, "Well, it's Amazon, and it's a billion greenback company. Surely, they will now not get out of commercial enterprise, so I think I will preserve just a piece longer." You ought to not do this. You must comply with the policies of your very own day trading strategy. You can quickly return to the trade; however, it could be tough to recover from a significant loss.

Get out once you are losing money, then promptly return as soon as the market is showing stability. Each time you alternate, you are exposing your money, so you need to limit this chance exposure. You must discover an appropriate set-up, then manipulate the danger with the right percentage length and stop loss.

Risk Management Is Important for Successful Day Trading

The best set-up is an opportunity with a purpose to get into an alternate with minimal hazard. This means you may risk $50; however, you can make $150. This is a 3:10 profit-loss ratio.

Meanwhile, if you get into a set-up in which you're risking $50 to make $5, then you have a less than one danger-praise ratio, and that is a trade that you need to avoid. Seasoned day investors will no longer take the deals with a profit-to-loss rate of less than 2:1.

This manner, in case you purchase $500 stocks, and you are risking $50 on it, you must sell it for at the least $six hundred to make at the least $100. Indeed, if the rate comes down to $400, you ought to accept the loss and exit the marketplace with only $400 ($50 damage).

If you aren't capable of discovering an exact set-up with the correct profit-to-loss ratio, then try to flow on and keep searching out any other trade. As a day trader, you should always search for opportunities to gain low chance entries with significant win potential.

Part of the studying procedure in day trading is the capability to become aware of set-ups that have a significant capacity for winning. As a novice in this area, you could discover it challenging to identify unique set-ups. It can be tough to be able to perceive a false breakout from a home run. This is something that you may develop through revel in and training.

Using a 2:1 win-loss ratio, there's a risk that you can be incorrect 40% of the time. However, you could still make money. Again, your task as a day trader is to manipulate hazards, no longer merely to buy and promote stocks. Your selected broker will cope with the transaction of trading. Your primary obligation is to manage the dangers.

Whenever you buy stocks, you're exposing money to risk. How can you manipulate this? There are three steps you need to don't forget so that it will manage danger. You want to decide if you are trading the proper stock.

We will learn how to locate the proper stocks for day trading. We will discuss in detail a way to find stocks which can be best for day investors, and what criteria you need to look for in them.

You should consider the following:

- Avoid stocks that are mainly traded by using institutional traders and algorithmic traders.

- Avoid stocks that have a small relative trading volume.

- Avoid penny stocks that might be genuinely manipulated.

- Avoid stocks that are moving without fresh fundamental catalysts.

Bear in thoughts that hazard control starts evolved from deciding on the right sort of stock to exchange. You could have an excellent platform and tools, and turn out to be professional in day trading strategies. But you'll genuinely lose cash if you are trading the wrong stocks.

You also need to decide an appropriate share length you must take. Are 10 stocks enough? Is it advocated to take 100 stocks? How about 1000 stocks? This all relies upon on the scale of your account as well as your day by day target.

If you're targeting $1,000 per day, then 10 to twenty stocks will suffice. You can see either growth your account size or take more fabulous stocks.

You can also need to decrease your daily purpose in case you don't have enough money to alternate for a $1,000 day by day target.

I am maintaining around $25,000 in my trading account, and I usually pick out 800 stocks to trade. My day by day purpose is $500 or $120,000/year. That is enough for my lifestyle.

What Is Your Trading Aim? What Is Your Stop Loss?

If you have got a small account, it is satisfactory to trade fewer stocks at first. When you notice an attractive exchange, however, you need to vicinity a logical stop in which better than 2% of your capital is at risk, then you ought to pass on that exchange, and move on to find every other one.

Always recognize your threat tolerance, and many profitable traders don't chance more significant than 2% in their capital on an unmarried trade.

Three Steps in Managing Risks

Here are the three steps you could take to manipulate your dangers effectively:

Step 1 - Figure out the maximum dollar threat for the trade you're planning. Take notice that this should not be better than the 2% of your account. Make sure which you have calculated this earlier than you begin you is a trading day. For example, permit's say that you have a $20,000 account. With the 2% rule, you may only risk $400 for an unmarried exchange. If you need to be extra conservative, you can restrict yourself to trading $200 each transfer or 1% of your account.

Step 2 - Estimate your max threat according to the proportion and prevent-loss approach. Let's say which you are looking at the stock of BBRY (Blackberry) the usage of ABCD Pattern Strategy. You buy stocks at $eight and want to promote it at $11, with a prevent loss at $6.50. You might be risking $1.50 / proportion.

Step 3 - Find the maximum wide variety of stocks you need to alternate. You can do this by dividing one using 2. Following the examples above, you will be allowed to buy the simplest 133 stocks or rounded to 125 shares.

You can only remember max loss on your account, depending on your account size. So you want to make that name for yourself. For instance, if you prevent is better than you're moving ordinary, you need to make some calculations and test if this prevents is greater than the maximum account size. If the ruin of moving familiar will yield a $300 loss, and you've set a $2 hundred max loss every trade, then you need to cancel the alternate or take a decrease quantity of stocks.

You might imagine that it can be tough to compute percentage length or forestall loss relying on a max loss in your account, even as you're anticipating the proper opportunity. You need to make rapid selections, or you may lose the possibility. It is additionally real that computing your stop loss and max loss on your account size in a stay trade isn't always commonly accessible.

Let me take you back to rule no. 2: day trading is hard. You need to exercise, and it is suitable for newbie traders to practice underneath supervision for at least three months in a simulated account. Through this, you may discover ways to manipulate your account in addition to your risk for each alternate. Gradually, you can without difficulty discern out the numbers by using yourself.

Risk Management and Trading Psychology

Day trading is often tricky, and a lot of new investors fail. It calls for sound option-making abilities, in addition to strong self-discipline. When you learned that an investor had taken a stake in Tesla, your initial reaction might be to sign up for the trend. However, you want to make a fast option whether or not you ought to buy or promote or sell short Tesla stocks. You can efficaciously do this with the subject.

Your trading techniques will gradually improve over time. But as early as now, you need to recognize that the key to earning money in day trading is to manipulate yourself and exercise self-subject. It may be hard to be expecting the stock marketplace behavior, and in case you don't recognize what you'll do, you could lose the game.

You want to stand in your own feet as even the maximum superior trading tools can't help a dealer who doesn't know what to do. You want to ask the following questions:

Is this particular route of action healthy for my trading strategy? What trading strategy will this movement fit into? If this alternate is going awry, in which do I prevent? How much cash am I risking in the alternate, and what is the ability praise?

This fact is what many day buyers discover tough. The selection-making method in day trading is typically a hard multitasking call. On top of that, you could experience the pressure.

Chapter 6. Best Time to Day Trade

Forex trading styles are majorly categorized depending on the length of time that the trader holds a position and expects it to win. Some traders prefer to hold positions for weeks, while others would prefer to hold for minutes or even hours.

Day trading refers to the short-term trading style where a trader closes a transaction within the day without holding it overnight. In most cases, the trader takes trades for a day and closes it as soon they hit the target any time before the day is over. The traders act on their bias and pick a side at the beginning of the day, and at the end of the day, they close with a profit or loss. Day traders do not like holding the trades overnight. This style of trade is best suited for people who have enough time in a day to analyze, monitor, and execute a trade within a day.

One can be a forex day trader if he/she likes to initiate and end a trade within a day, has enough time to closely monitor the market trends throughout the day, especially in the morning, and likes to know if he/she won or lost within a trading day. If one does not have enough time to analyze the markets throughout or for the better part of the day, has a day job that requires too much attention, or likes longer or shorter-term trading, then he/she might not be able to participate in day forex trade.

There are some things that one should consider before venturing into day trade; for instance, a trader should ensure that he /she has a means of staying updated on the latest basic events. The knowledge allows one to choose a direction and make decisions at the start of the day. If one has a full-time day job, they need to take serious considerations because it will be required of them to divide the time between work and trade. The person might get fired if he/she spends too much time looking at the charts during office hours.

There are different types of day trading, including Trend trading, Countertrend trending, and Break out trading. Trend trading involves situations where the trader observes a longer time frame chart and determines the overall trend. After that, the trader moves to a smaller time frame chart and analyses the trading opportunity following the trend.

The trader uses the indicators on the shorter frame to get an idea of when they should time their entries. Countertrade, on the other hand, has worked like trend trading, but the trader looks for opportunities in the opposite direction after observing the overall trend. The idea behind countertrend trading is to identify the end of a trend and make an early entry when the trend reverses. Countertrend trading is riskier, but a trader can have huge profits when used correctly.

Break out trading refers to the situations where a trader looks at the range made by a particular pair during certain day hours then placing a trade on either side while hoping to get a breakout. Breakout trading is particularly good when the pair has been in a tight range because that indicates that the pair will make a big move in a short while.

The goal of the trader in the breakout trading is to position him/herself strategically such that once the move occurs, he/she catches the wave. In the breakout trading method, the trader determines the range where resistance and supports have been holding strongly, then setting the entry points either below or above the breakout levels. The rule of thumb in this trading is to target an equal amount of pips, making up the determined range.

Practical Strategies for Day Trading

Day traders follow the events that lead to short term market changes. One popular technique that the day traders rely on is trading the news. Market psychology and market expectations identify that markets react to scheduled announcements such as corporate earnings, economic statistics, and interest rates. Markets drastically react when the set expectations are exceeded, or the expectations have not been met, and the significant price movements can benefit day traders very much.

Day traders also use the fade the gap technique to get benefits within a short period. When a trader observes a gap between the day's opening and the closing of the previous day, he/she may take a position in the opposite direction, therefore, closing the gap. During the day when there is no news, gaps are rare. However, the traders still take a view on the direction that the market is generally moving. If a trader anticipates that the market will move up, he/she may buy securities that display strength when their prices fall. In the cases where the trader observes a downward trend in the market, he/she may sell the securities that show weaknesses when the prices bounce. Many independent day traders use short days, whereby they work for 2 to 5 hours per day only.

In many cases, the traders will practice their trade skills on a demo account before going live. Demo accounts help the traders to track the failures and successes compared with the markets. Therefore, they learn through experience.

Manage Your Day Trading Risk

The foreign exchange market is very extensive and has very few barriers to entry. Consequently, it is one of the most open markets across the globe, and anyone can access it from wherever. Theoretically speaking, if one can access the internet, it has a computer or a smartphone that supports trade and some money, and then he/she can start trading in the foreign exchange market. Many new entrants into foreign exchange start with day trading. However, the ease of entry does not represent the ease of making profits, as many people assume. There are some common mistakes that day traders make leading to failure.

First, many traders fail to record their ratios. As a day trader, there are two identified statistics that one should keep an eye on; the risk /reward ratio and the win rate. A trader's win rate is the number of times a trader wins expressed as a percentage. For instance, if the trader wins 80 times out of 100, then the win rate is 80%. A day trader should maintain at least a 50%-win rate. The risk-reward ratio represents the number of wins concerning the number of losses an average trade. For example, if a trader loses an average of $500 and wins an average of $750, then the risk/reward ratio is $750/$500= 1.5. A trader should ensure that he/she keeps the risk/reward ratio above 1 to minimize loss. Ideally, the best margin is 1.25, and this indicates a profitable trader. In some cases, a trade can still be profitable when the win rate is lower, and the reward ratio is higher and vice versa.

The second common mistake made by day traders involves trading without a stop loss. A stop loss is to offset a trade if the prices move against the trader to a certain extent. The trader selects the amount at which the order should get him/her out of the trade. A stop-loss order moderates' loss, and it's very helpful for beginner traders.

The third mistake that the day traders make involves adding to losing day trade. Many traders tend to average down when losses occur with the hope that the trend will reverse.

Averaging down refers to the process of adding to a position while the prices are moving against the trader. This is a dangerous practice because the price can move against the trader for longer than expected, therefore causing exponential loss. Instead of risking everything, one should take a trade and set a stop-loss order such that once the price hits the set target, the trade is automatically closed.

Fourthly, some trades risk more than they can afford to lose. The key strategy of forex trading is identifying the amount of capital one is willing to lose if the deal goes wrong. Ideally, a day trader should risk a maximum of 1 percent of their capital in any one trade.

As such, the set stop-loss order should close trade of it leads to more than 1 percent loss in trading capital. Consequently, this will mean that when a trader loses multiple trades consistently, only a very small amount of capital will be lost. Again, the trader can make 2 or 3 percent on each win, therefore, covering the losses very easily.

Another capital risk management strategy is controlling the losses daily. Instead of using one stop-loss order for several days, a trader should select a stop order for every day. Some days are worse than others; therefore, a trader can lose a substantial amount of capital in one day. A daily stop loss is very important to mitigate risks.

Many traders also make the mistake of going all-in. Even when they have identified good strategies to mitigate loss, the traders are sometimes tempted to ignore the signs and take too large a trade than they normally would.

The reasons for going all-in depend on the intention of the trader and the purpose of the trade. For example, a trader may have experienced a tremendous amount of losses in a row of trades. Therefore, he/she seeks to recuperate. Again, a trader might have done so well for a while that they feel like they cannot lose.

Day Trading for a Living and Options

In some cases, trades look so appealing, and the trader becomes too confident about a win, therefore, places more than the set strategy. It is best if a trader sticks to his/ her trade rule, such as a 1 percent risk per trade and a 3 percent risk per day. If one risks too much capital, they might make a mistake, and in most cases, mistakes tend to accumulate and augment.

When the risk fails to pay off, a trader may cancel his/her stop order with the hope that the trade will turn around. In other cases, a trader will be tempted to add to the position, still hoping that the trade gone wrong will turn around. To avoid such temptations, it is best if the trader identifies a risk management strategy and sticks to it without going all in.

Beginner traders also try to participate in the news because it seems like a pleasant way of making a profit. Many trade pairs fall and rise sharply to reflect the news released to the world about the economy. Many traders, especially the experienced ones, identify the possible movements in the trade based on the news and take a position before the information hits the market. In some cases, it is a good way to make quick profits, but some cases end up in extensive losses.

Chapter 7. The Biggest Day Trading Mistakes

The great toggle game has become even more exciting. With active day trading sessions, traders make quick profits (and losses) in a short period. A little knowledge is a dangerous thing. With proper knowledge, discipline, and an alternative-based approach, you, too, can win the prize (and set the goal) in the markets.

The Downside

While most traders try to prevent this from happening, it inevitably does. The first is that you maintain a losing posture that is costly not only in terms of time but also in terms of effort and money. A better position is a step up the commercial scale, and day trading is about anticipating gains (and losses) before they occur. For every dollar lost, higher capital returns are needed to report losses.

For example, for a sustained 50% loss, you must make a 100% profit to balance things out. Reducing the average in such a situation can lead to significant losses or margins. This is because trends can remain unchanged even when traders are more liquid; therefore, if capital is added as the position comes out of the winning gains.

Day traders must be wary of how news is moving in the market and where the trend is going—taking a position before an ad can harm a trader's chances of success. There is no easy money; it's about working hard and thinking smart.

Don't Trade Right After the News

A news headline can reach markets that are beginning to move quickly. This does not necessarily mean that you will earn money. If you don't have a solid trading plan, then you are simply gambling. News announcements lead to panic reactions and emotional responses, something that really hurts the day trade.

Wait for Volatility to Decrease

Day traders need to ensure that volatility decreases and that there is a clear trend towards development after the news is published. Fewer liquidity problems, more efficient management of resources is possible. Therefore, a stable price direction is likely.

Don't Risk more than You Can Afford to Lose

Regardless of the time, traders should not risk more than 1% of capital within a single transaction. Professional traders risk less than 1% of capital. Day trading also involves additional attention to the maximum day risk to be implemented. The maximum day risk may be approximately 1 percent or less of capital and is equal to the average daily profit over one month, for example. By using maximum risk, traders ensure that they do not risk more than they can afford to lose.

Accept that the Market May Be Illogical

Trading expectations are usually imposed on the market. We think in terms of what we want rather than the right trading address. The market is not interested in what a person needs. In the short, long and medium-term, markets can be volatile or modern depending on trading conditions.

Accept how the market behaves. Remember that capital growth over time may be accompanied by an increase in the size of the position to achieve higher dollar returns. New strategies can be implemented with minimal capital to get started. Therefore, new strategies can yield positive results. As time increases and the trading day progresses, the strategy may need to be changed.

Entering a Trading Day without a Plan Can Be Disastrous

Loss protection means regulating the input-output and, above all, escaping the price or stopping the loss. Here you have some advice to take into account:

- Don't leave margins out.

- Trade with the money you have, not the money you borrowed.

- Don't try to chase the trades.

- A common mistake during the day trading is to chase trading.

- Failure to understand markets or limit orders can have consequences.

There is always a game between the market and the limit order. Although the market order is an order to buy or sell shares at current market rates, the limit order allows you to set the maximum or minimum price for commercial security. Market orders can be processed quickly, but the market should not control the order. Similarly, limited orders can allow verification of parameters. If limited orders or market orders make sense to you, you should be clear that you cannot lose a fast-moving stock to save some bucks. High-quality stocks that are liquid allow the use of a market or a limited order.

Adhere to Suggestions, Pay the Price

In what may seem contradictory, it is important to remember that whoever wants to help you does not have to be your best friend. Market experts often have plans, and nothing comes close to fair trade. Today's successful traders think about what they want to deduce and judge accordingly. They are not influenced by what others think.

Refusing to Cut Losses Can Be Costly

Human nature is intrinsically full of hope, and it means that traders could expect a change. It can be a fatal mistake. Refusing to cut losses can damage your account. If your stock heads south, there is no need to continue with it on a trip anywhere. Avoid turning small losses into larger losses.

Timing Is Everything in Day Trade

Trading too early or too late, too little, or too much can be disastrous.

Remember that the first few minutes of trading are always confusing, and the competition towards the closing or opening bell is always with institutional investors and high-frequency trading experts, in other words, the big fish in the sea. When the indicators become unstable, be sure to retract.

Discipline Is Everything

Discipline is actually what it takes to be a successful day trader. Develop strict rules and don't trust emotions. Day traders can also use technical analysis. For example, stochastics can be used to plot a graph if a stock is trading above or below.

Beginning Traders Seek Magic; Experts Know Best

Don't look for a magic bullet or miracle in the day trading, because there is none. Reading charts is as important as listening to the news, and there is no easy way to play in the markets. It takes strategy and discipline to make sure you are making a profit.

Uninformed Traders Lack Knowledge

A day trader should not think that someone can make money in the markets. To be successful, you need training.

A constantly winning trader starts with paper trading and studies it long enough to discover how the market works. Going through the day trading education can be as intense and comprehensive as a Ph.D. course! A day trade is about taming the lion

Making money with small variations in the price of security requires skill and deep understanding. High-speed Internet connections and a lot of nervousness can ensure that day trading is easy to do. But it is also important to have a strong and confident approach. Just as an animal can perceive fear, so can a market.

Develop a Trading Plan

Day trading strategies are a business proposition like producing income. Trading plans should include a list of the equipment needed to succeed and a projection of minimum profitability in the short and long term. Keeping track of your budget wouldn't be a bad idea, either. This includes a record of day trading expenses.

Have a Solid Day Trading Philosophy

You should identify performance benchmarks and discover which strategies work best for you during the trading day.

This includes defining what gives you an advantage over others, identifying the trade you are trying to start, and defining the exit strategy.

Consider the Losses

In day trading, you can't have a perfect batting average.

Follow a Trading Strategy

It is easy to bite the bullet and get caught up in emotions. This can lead to dangerous trading activities, such as impulse selling or buying.

You must devise a trading strategy that promises success, not a failure. More importantly, you need to keep emotions out of the equation.

Don't Change the Strategy too Often

Many times, day traders change a strategy because it doesn't seem to work. They don't consider external factors such as market dynamics or volatility. This is your obstacle.

Use the News

Take a look at the financial news reports so you can understand what is happening on the day markets. Analyze each trade in the context of the news you receive and choose profitable, successful trades.

Keep a Trading Journal

A trading journal can help you manage your profit and loss in an organized way. You can even keep an electronic journal if you find it easier.

Always Do a Post-trade Analysis

You must adapt to changing markets, and this is only possible if you change your strategies accordingly. The changing dynamics and intrinsic volatility of the market must be understood, not feared. Therefore, use a stop loss with each order to avoid bad trade. Use limit orders well and don't follow the trend, instead look for stable returns. Not knowing what point to capitalize in the markets is perhaps the biggest problem in day trading. The use of the principles of psychology or behavioral finance is important. You need to know what

Chapter 8. Competition with Bank Traders

Sales and Trading (S&T) is a division at an asset bank that contains salespeople who call proposals and opportunities from institutional investors, and traders who execute orders and advise clients to enter and exit economic positions. Sales and transaction is the essence that makes or disrupts a financial investment company, whether it's a stock exchange, a hedge endowment, or an asset bank. If the company can't sell its services to customers effectively, then it can't do business – and if it can't trade well, it becomes impossible for the company to get and retain customers and make profits.

Sales Accomplishments

One of the main activities in selling and trading is investment transactions. At an investment company, the salespeople convey equity material to investors. Sales employees track market news such as periodical earnings reports or union/attainment material in tandem with the trading staff of the investment firm to alert them to specific investment prospects that they can sell on to potential investors.

Sales supervisors play a particularly important role in the initial public offerings (I.P.O.s) performed by an asset bank. When an asset bank takes over the role of managing a new stock's first issue, they agree to sell a defined number of shares at a quantified minimum price. The asset bank must be confident that its salespeople will successfully sell the requisite number of shares in the secondary market, either to institutional or individual investors, to prevent the need to buy part of the stock contribution themselves. A large part of what makes an investment bank competitive can sell shares effectively. To this end, the sales staff is constantly establishing relationships with potential buyers of shares, such as pension funds, portfolio directors of mutual funds, and other main official buyers.

In addition to calling clients, the salespeople in an investment firm are also in constant contact with portfolio executives and other trading staff to get appropriate market info and to know the investments are focused on by the trading staff.

In a traditional stock brokerage business involved in sales and trading, the brokers are the salespeople who approach potential investors – whether individual or official – and try to persuade them to invest money with the firm. Brokers may also serve as dealers, or may not. Nonetheless, the more common method is to handle brokers bringing in investment capital, which is then handled by the trading staff.

Mutual Endowment, ETF, and Hedge Fund Trading

In many fields of financial selling and trading, investment companies offering mutual funds or exchange-traded funds (ETF) do not sell to I.P.O.s but still have to hire successful sales staff. Sales staff in organizations like Fidelity Investments is tasked with attracting customers to the different funds sold by Fidelity, Vanguard, or other related firms. Mutual funds and ETFs make money by paying a premium that is a percentage of the fund's overall asset volume. Therefore the more creditors and the greater quantity of investment wealth, the company will entice to upsurge the income of the corporation.

Trades of hedge fund reserves can differ considerably in terms of who is doing the vending and who are possible investors. For a new hedge fund happening by a new hedge endowment manager, the hedge fund manager who does the vending is also the sole salesclerk of the fund, at least in the beginning. It happens before they find enough investors and produce enough income to employ a salesperson and assign the sales job to them. As possible investors, hedge funds also vary in how they behave. Many hedge funds object institutional investors while others quintessence on raising investment wealth from high net worth people (H.N.W.I.) who have vast sums of money to invest in.

Sales

The sales job is essentially intimately linked to trading jobs. This is because the sales staff's ultimate task, irrespective of the type of financial firm they hire, is to persuade prospective customers that the traders of the company are better than traders working for rival financial firms. A stockbroker is seeking to convince clients that the brokerage company provides superior sales and trading research and analysis. A hedge endowment manager tries to encourage investors that he or she will attain higher investment revenues. Salespeople at an asset bank advertise the ability of the bank to get the maximum amount of money for an I.P.O., or the aptitude of the bank to bargain the most effective buying and sales services for big, institutional depositors.

Trading Operations

Traders buy and sell stocks as a share of sales and trading practices, either on behalf of the investment corporation for which they operate or on behalf of their customers. Investment firms have a variety of traders specializing in numerous zones of investment, such as stocks, shares, or commodities. Specialization of vending and exchange usually goes much deeper than for individual traders assigned to, for example, simply trade in the gold market or trade-in a particular business sector such as healthcare or transport.

Traders are accountable for risk and resource management as well as safety research. In major large trading companies, such as asset banks, traders also participate in selling and trading with their peers in other investment firms or commercial banks due to the large number of shares that they usually sell at one time.

Two Elementary Forms of Trading

Agency trading and exclusive trading, more commonly referred to as prop trading, are both similar, different types of trading.

Agency traders behave to clients as a trading agent (hence the name). Their role is to conduct trades as skillfully as conceivable on behalf of the customers of the company. The skillful execution of trade is particularly relevant for traders at asset banks doing business for clients of institutional investors. There is no artificial way to buy 50 or 100 shares of a given stock. Still, when a depositor wants to purchase 100,000 or a million stocks, they need to allocate their purchase deliberately so that they can obtain the required amount of shares at a reasonable price without making their purchase push up the price.

Unlike agency traders, prop traders are not dealing on behalf of investment investors but are instead in charge of selling their own money from the financial firm. For example, a prop trader at a profitable bank might trade the foreign exchange (forex) market to maximize the value of the bank's resources. Prop traders have the right to trade that the agency traders do not; however, risk limits set by the investment firm also restrict them.

The third category of trader, a flow trader, is somewhat of a cross between an agency trader and a prop trader. Flow Traders will be trading concurrently on behalf of clienteles and behalf of the investment firm if, for example, a customer wants to purchase parts of a stock which the investment firm owns and desires to trade. The flow trader makes the transaction on behalf of the customer but also acts as an agent for the company by selling the customer shares, which the investment firm holds.

Although knowing the basic forms of trading is significant, it is also vital to bear in mind that terms such as agency trading and prop trading are just general descriptions. That kind of trading is frequently, not as simply black and white, as such differences.

Trading Various Securities

Traders Groups are usually discriminated not only by in what way they trade-agency or prop trading-but by what they trade. In an asset or commercial bank, traders are divided into separate classes that manage the trading of numerous types of securities, such as fixed-income tools, impartialities, commodities, or foreign exchange.

The emergence of financial byproducts such as collateralized debt obligations (C.D.O.s) and difference contracts (C.F.D.s) both widened trading groups and somewhat blurred the limits between groups. For example, C.D.O.s fall into the overall arrangement of fixed-income instruments. Still, because they are byproducts, they can be exchanged distinctly by traders precisely assigned to trading extras or exchanged by the normal fixed-income trading division of a company.

Traders concentrate on the trading of different instruments inside each core trading grouping (e.g., fixed income, impartialities, and commodities). For instance, the fixed-income trading division of a company would have traders assigned to commercial government bonds, corporate bonds, and other debt-related instruments. Trading securities can also skill traders within specified ranges of maturity, such as trading bonds with experiences of 10 years or less.

How to Turn into a Specialized Trader

Take Your Swapping to the Subsequent Level

To become a Professional Trader, you need to know the basics of trading and advanced fundamentals. When these are learned, you will be able to learn tested techniques and gain expertise in their execution.

It's also necessary to be practical about the career. There is no perfect trading method that consistently only yields winning results. Nevertheless, if you practice how to differentiate from what is wrong or deceptive to accurate information, you will spend much of your time concentrating on the knowledge that will make you a more effective and successful trader.

Trading Fundamentals

Learning business and trading fundamentals are some of the most effective strategies for learning to trade. A strong understanding of the fundamentals provides the foundation that will sustain your entire career. Until more advanced trading information can be effectively applied, this first level of knowledge is needed.

The fundamentals include all the factual trading details, such as:

- The markets to trade

- How prices change (bid and request prices)

- Order forms and how to position them

- Risk organization

- Trading periods

- How to path trading efficiency

- How much wealth is needed to trade effectively?

Trading fundamentals are usually factual, and there is not much subjectivity. One source of information might entitle that currency or forex trading starts with at least $500, while another source may claim that it starts with at least $1,000. One source is no right or wrong. Multiple source information suggests you should certainly start with at least $500, and rather with $1,000 or more.

The markets themselves have the most significant market circumstances for traders. The New York Stock Exchange and NASDAQ, for example, offer enlightening tools about how the stock market works through the key menus about their websites. The Chicago Mercantile Exchange is doing that for futures, and the Chicago Board Options Exchange is doing the same for those who want to know about trading in stocks.

Knowing the Advanced Fundamentals

Knowing Trading fundamentals offer new traders a chance to learn about the various markets and the one they want to trade-in. Traders decide whether they want to sell stocks, futures, options, or forex trading while learning the fundamentals. They may then dig further into the trade conditions unique to that market while making this option.

New options trader, for example, needs to know about Greek options, which help decide the price of an option. All who are interested in futures trading need to know about ticks, points, and the various requirements they may want to exchange for each futures contract. During regular hours, stock traders need to know how to sell short, how dividends operate, and the variations between pre-market trading and trading. Forex traders need to know about pip prices and roll-over rates every day.

Chapter 9. What is Swing Trading?

The concept of swing trading is deceptively simple. All it means is that you buy and sell stocks or other investments to make short-term profits. In other words, swing trading seeks to profit from short-term price movements on the stock market (or other markets such as currency trading). However, unlike day trading, the price movements we are interested in last from days to weeks or possibly up to a couple of months or so.

It differs from day trading in one key aspect. Swing trading involves holding securities overnight, possibly for weeks at a time. Therefore, you can be looking for short-term swings in the price of a stock, for example. However, you aren't looking for that swing in price to occur for a single day, but rather over a few days, or weeks. Some people who swing trade can even lengthen that time out to a couple of months or so. You might even say you are a swing trader if your strategy is to hold stocks for several months but buy low and sell high over that period.

How Does Swing Trading Differ from Day Trading?

Firstly, let's make an observation. You cannot day trade without making it a full-time living. Starting from some first principles, a day trade is one that opens and closes the position on the same day. You might only hold the stock for a few hours or even for a matter of minutes.

From this definition, you can understand that you need to be paying strict attention to the movements of the stock or security on a moment-by-moment basis. The first thing you do with day trading is you need to know the exact right moment to buy the stock. Of course, there are high odds that you will guess wrong (not that day traders "guess"). But what's working against you is that over the short term. However, traders do utilize a lot of analysis in their work, the stock market is essentially a chaotic system, with a lot of randomness built into it.

Secondly, there is the problem of what is the right moment to sell. Therefore, you need to know when to get out of the position at just the right time so that you're exiting and able to make good profits. That is a very tough and nerve-racking game to play.

Of course, there are many good methods that, if followed to the letter, can produce success in day trading. That is not something anyone is going to do on the fly and be successful. There may be that one person in a thousand that can do that, but most people are going to need extensive training. Even then, the reality is that most day, traders fail to make consistent profits, or even profit at all.

With swing trading, you're looking to profit on price moves, but it's a far more relaxed method. If things are not working out for you on any given day, you can wait it out.

To be a day trader, the vast majority of brokerages are going to require that you have $25,000 in your account. That doesn't necessarily have to be $25,000 in cash; it could be a $25,000 combination of cash and stocks. That said, it's a significant barrier to entry for many people. Even people who have $25,000 on hand may not want to risk it all on a few day trades.

There are a couple of brokerages that don't have this requirement, and they allow you to day trade with any amount of funds. However, they charge massive commissions. Those may be suitable to learn on, and you can even profit. But professional traders don't use them because of the high commissions, and you probably wouldn't want to stick with them long term if you find out you have a knack for day trading and can make profits from it.

Day trading as a defined category goes well beyond what brokerages think; it's a matter of law and even taxes.

There are strict legal definitions that were created by the United States government that say exactly what a day trader is. The first part of the definition to be aware of is that you are going to be labeled a day trader if you enter into four-day trades within any five days. Just to be clear, a day trade is defined as buying and selling the same security on the same trading day.

A swing trader, in contrast, is someone that is going to hold the position at least overnight. Swing traders may hold a position for several days, weeks, and even out to a few months in time. A swing trader simply holds his positions for a far longer amount of time than a day trader does.

Secondly, there are no capital requirements imposed on swing traders. If you have five dollars in your account and buy a share of a stock that is five dollars a share, you can swing trade that one share of stock.

The only requirement for swing trading is that you have the capital available that you need for your personal goals (and any requirements that your broker has to open an account if any). Of course, buying one share of a five-dollar stock isn't going to get you anywhere financially, but the point is swing trading isn't an official designation to the point that day trading is. As far as the broker is concerned, a swing trader isn't any different from any other investor.

When you are buying a stock traditionally, you will do so based on the fundamentals of the company. What that means, in a nutshell, is that you're going to be looking at the recent history of revenues and profits ("recent" being over the past five years), the management team, price to earnings ratio, and whether or not the stock is undervalued. You would also be looking at the company's long-term prospects, as well as its history. What are the products it is coming out? Is it engaged in R&D? Will it be expanding into new markets? Fundamentals mean looking at something for long-term investment and getting into the business that the company is engaged in.

Day traders are not concerned with the fundamentals of a company. That could come into play at times, like on a day when a company has an earnings call. For a day trader, the concern is based on how the stock is moving over a few minutes or hours. This fact may have absolutely nothing to do with fundamentals, or, as our example of an earnings call illustrates, it could be related to it. The point is: fundamentals are of prime concern for long-term investors, but it's an unrelated or fleeting issue for day traders.

So, in short, a swing trader kind of takes a middle ground between the two extremes of day trading and long-term investing.

As a swing trader, you will be paying attention to technical analysis, but it won't take as central a role as it does in day trading. Secondly, while day traders pay relatively little attention to fundamental analysis, generally speaking, a swing trader is going to be much more interested in the fundamentals of the company. But not quite as focused as a Warren Buffett who looks at long time horizons.

How Does Swing Trading Differ from Buy and Hold Investing?

Most people come to the stock market, thinking about traditional buy-and-hold investing. Buy-and-hold investing is a technique that is focused on the long-term gains of the stock market and highly valued companies.

If you invest in specific companies at all, and many people don't, a buy-and-hold investor is looking for high-quality buys. Its true investing, meaning that you're focused on the fundamentals of the company and its long-term prospects, and you are putting your money into the market to invest in the company over the long-term, which can mean up to 30 years or more.

The buy-and-hold investor is going to dig into a company very deeply when it comes to the fundamentals. That means going over the financial statements and cash flow in detail, seeing how things are changing year to year, and reading all the earnings reports and following the calls. It also means studying the management team, including who they are and what is in their backgrounds. You are going to familiarize yourself with the company's products and what markets they are in.

A good buy-and-hold investor that invests in specific companies will approach it as if a friend or relative said: "hey, do you want to invest in my business?" Buy-and-hold investors have low turnover rates in their portfolios. Some buy-and-hold investors are income or dividend investors, hoping to make a living off dividend payments either now or in the future, while safely preserving their capital.

They may be inclined to invest in a slowly changing stock like Chevron or IBM, as opposed to some stock that sees significant price swings over days, weeks, or months.

Many buy-and-hold investors these days don't even invest in individual companies. With the advent of exchange-traded funds, it's possible to buy and sell shares on the stock market while investing in index funds rather than investing in individual companies or being constrained by stodgy and expensive mutual funds.

Given that an index like the S&P 500 is going to go up over the long term barring some unforeseen disaster, a simple buying and hold strategy is to load up on index funds like SPY. Of course, the most extreme buy-and-hold investor would be someone who invests in mutual funds, and they let the fund manager keep track of all the investments and rarely check on it themselves. Such investors just hope to have a "nest egg" in retirement.

Regardless of whether a buy-and-hold or long-term investor invests in specific companies, index funds, mutual funds, or some combination out of all of these, they will use the same basic techniques.

Those techniques involve diversification of your portfolio and using methods like dollar-cost averaging. They will also be looking for so-called value stocks, which are undervalued at present based on the fundamentals of the company. So the investor hopes to make cheap buys of quality stocks that will appreciate over the long term.

We see that, right off the bat, buy-and-hold investing is quite different from swing trading. Swing trading does pay some attention to the fundamentals of the company, but the focus remains on short-term profits. Even when looking at fundamentals, the swing trader is interested in how they are going to impact share prices in the coming weeks, not over decades.

Techniques like diversification are of limited interest to the swing trader. You will have a little bit of diversity in that, and you are going to be buying and selling multiple securities over time as you get involved with more trades simultaneously. Beginning swing traders may not have any diversity at all and may only be buying and selling one security at a time.

Dollar-cost averaging is not something a swing trader would consider at all. If you don't know what that means, dollar cost averaging is a strategy that uses investing at regular intervals. The idea is to average out the price paid for shares of stock as it fluctuates up and down. People who use dollar-cost averaging have a philosophy that over the long term, those price fluctuations are going to average out, and many believe you can't predict price fluctuations anyway (they might take a dim view of technical analysis).

Chapter 10. Why Is Leverage Riskier?

Another significant risk to be aware of is that of leverage. Because Options don't cost much as stock as they are simply a contract, this means that they experience disproportionately larger percentage price gains in reaction to the far more expensive underlying stock's very small price movements. The huge benefit of this is that it results in large percentage gains when the underlying stock moves in the anticipated direction by even a small amount. It is not necessarily an issue with beginners, or at least it shouldn't be as the risk manifests itself mainly through trading too large a position size. One simple way to nullify or minimize this level of risk is to keep your position size small.

Lastly, Options, as we know, possess a time value (extrinsic value) in addition to their inherent, intrinsic value (in the money value), which is also another double-edged sword. For option buyers, time-decay acts as a headwind because it is continually decreasing the value of the option. By doing so, this increases the dependency on greater stock price movement to break even on the trade. For option writers, it acts as a tailwind because it allows a profit to be generated through steady premium incomes regardless of whether the stock moves or not.

The Advantages of Leverage in Options Trading

The options exchanges play a critical role in ensuring that there are enough securities to base options contracts on. The following are some of the significant functions of an options exchange (VAIDYA, 2017).

Liquidity

Perhaps the biggest function of options exchanges is to ensure ready markets for options contracts. The markets ensure that holders of options can exercise their options and that there are enough buyers to purchase the options. Traders are looking for avenues to increase their earning potential, and liquidity helps them achieve that. Options contracts have a time limit, unlike other securities such as shares, which necessitates liquidity. The existence of market makers is particularly responsible for liquidity.

Gauging a Country's Economy

The state of an options market can reliably inform us what the country's economic situation is like. The most common underlying assets that traders base their options on our shares. The prevailing economic conditions are always reflected in the share prices of various companies. If the country is experiencing prosperity, the share prices will be up, and if the country is experiencing market crashes, the share prices will go down. Thus, the options exchanges play a critical role in ensuring that traders have a sense of how their country is performing economy-wise. Stocks are the pulse of an economy, and they are accurate predictors of a country's economic state.

Securities Pricing

Options traders have a wide pool to choose from when it comes to underlying assets. However, the value of an underlying asset is determined by the options exchange according to the forces of demand and supply. The financial securities of prosperous companies are worth more than the securities of moderately successful companies. The valuation of securities is important not only for traders but also for governments. Governments levy taxes on earnings drawn from options trading, so they first have to get the value of the securities.

Safety of Transactions

Traders want to be sure that they can trust all the parties that they are getting into business with. Therefore, it is the work of an options exchange to ensure the players are trustworthy. For one, most options contracts are based on financial securities of publicly listed companies, and these companies must operate within stringent rules and regulations. Thus, the trader is assured of security when dealing with other parties. The options markets should provide all relevant information about options contracts and securities to discourage the trader from making a move out of ignorance.

Providing Speculation Scope

Speculation of securities is critical to ensure a healthy balance of demand and supply of securities. Many traders earn their profits from purely speculative risk. They have developed a skill of determining the movement of prices. The options exchanges provide traders with the resources and tools of speculating on the securities performance, thus allowing traders to earn profits.

Promotes Investment Culture

Options exchanges are critical in promoting the culture of investing in valuable securities like the stock as opposed to unproductive assets such as precious metals. Traders have a wide selection of underlying securities to base their options contracts on; thus, they are not limited in the range of their strategies. A big saving and investment culture is critical for the economic advancement of a country.

The Continuous Market for Securities

Options exchanges allow traders to base their options on a wide range of underlying securities, and in case of any risks, traders are at liberty to switch from one security to the next. This is different from purchasing stocks wherein you are stuck with the consequences of poor decisions.

Capital Formation

Options exchanges promote the pooling together and redistribution of resources. The exchanges create a win-win situation for both sides. Companies raise capital when their stocks are publicly listed, and their securities act as the underlying. On the other hand, traders stand to benefit from the high earning potential and low-capital requirements for options contracts. So, options exchanges play a critical role in ensuring that the parties are in a position to generate capital.

Control Companies

The significance of transparency within the derivatives market cannot be overstated. If a trader has the misfortune of working with shady companies, they could easily lose their earnings. Options exchanges make it hard for shady companies to spoil the market. For instance, publicly-traded companies have to submit relevant documents and adhere to certain performance standards, as doing so will boost investor confidence. Companies that refuse to cooperate with exchanges are blacklisted from the market.

Fiscal and Monetary Policies

The fiscal policy and the monetary policy of the government must not hurt the players in the financial industry. Options exchanges facilitate the creation and execution of key policies that will govern the financial markets.

Proper Canalization of Wealth

Options are a great way of putting capital into great use, as opposed to having the capital just sitting around. Thus, the economy benefits from an injection of capital, which would otherwise have been inactive. The injection of capital into the economy promotes wealth distribution and fights off economic disgraces like unemployment.

Education Purposes

Options trading features complex processes. Even people who claim to understand options trading might be low-key deluded. Thus, the importance of education cannot be overstated. Many traders just get the hang of things and set about purchasing and selling options contracts, forgetting that it is critical first to educate one's self. Options exchanges provide a wealth of resources and information that are meant to enlighten traders. Empowered traders improve trading activity.

Disadvantages of Leverage in Options Trading

Again, I won't bore you with elaborate explanations of the disadvantages of options trading. Instead, here's another helpful list that clearly outlines why traders might choose to shy away from potential options trading opportunities:

- Options are time-sensitive investments. Yes, you can pick and choose options based on expiration dates, but you'll always be confined to a certain expiration date where you must choose to act or choose to exit.

- Successful options trading requires your attention and time. Without it, you risk losing out on potential profit-generating opportunities that come from buying or selling your call or put option at the right, most profitable time.

- Options are without a paper-trail. With stocks and bonds, for example, you'll receive some sort of paper certification regarding your investment. Options are "book-entry" investments, meaning you receive no paper certification that shows your claim to an option or your ownership of an option.

- You're working in the stock market, a highly volatile place where changes occur suddenly and dramatically. You'll need to be on constant alert, or at least hire a broker who will.

- You'll need to be in a somewhat stable financial situation before you can successfully trade. Establishing and frequently adding to some sort of "trading fund" before you begin your options, trading endeavors will somewhat remedy an unstable financial situation, however.

Two other option cost factors should be considered:

1. Costs associated with the trading process

2. Cost of exercising the stock

By understanding the basic cost structure for an option, you can see how options also add through leverage an element of risk, even though options also provide leverage at a reduced risk.

The fact that Option prices are partially based on probabilities complicates the matter. For stock options, you want to consider the likelihood that a particular option will be in-the-money before or at expiration, given the type of price movements the underlying stock has recently undergone. The way an Option is valued takes into consideration six factors; Stock price, strike price, time to expiration, interest rates, and dividends, but there is a wildcard factor – volatility.

How to Manage Risk in Options Trading

Some folks are terrified of ever getting in the derivatives trading market, lamenting whose is often a very risky pursuit, but that's not necessarily true. Of course, you will find instances when options can be risky, yet you can also find situations wherein options can assist you in minimizing risk. It all comes as a result of the method that you utilize them. Options take less financial commitment than equities, and they're also resistant to the negative effects of gap openings.

A justified reason to go with buying options is always that you may be capable of limiting your risk right down to just the quantity of greenbacks that you pay to the premium. With other investment options, you may turn out losing a lot of cash, even money that you did not invest, to begin with, but it doesn't happen if you are working with options.

Let's state that you saw how the prices of cows were going to rise. You could pay some cash upfront and get into a binding agreement with another person to trade your five cows for $2,000. At this time, since you are utilizing an options contract, you did not find the cows upfront.

On the other hand, if you had risen towards the one else and purchased those cows straight up to get a price of $10,000, you could wind up in trouble. For this example, the retail price from the cows may end up falling by $500, instead of going up by $500, so you would wind up losing $2,500 inside the process. Since you went to the options contract though, you'd probably stand to lose a maximum of $250 if the prices were to fall afterward. You still are in a position to lose some money; however, it can be a lot less than you could have lost otherwise.

How to Trade Smarter Using Leverage

While investing is a rapidly growing hobby for some traders, it's a career for other traders. Despite your trading situation, however, you'll need to enter the options trading arena with the understanding that you'll be just one of thousands and thousands of traders seeking to generate a substantial profit through options trading.

Chapter 11. Know the Greeks

When it comes to trading options successfully, you must understand the multiple types of risks that come into play. To make them easier to discuss in detail, they have been broken down into different variables, each of which is labeled with a letter of the ancient Greek alphabet. Trading without taking the time to learn this valuable way to avoid as much risk as possible is akin to driving in a foreign country without first learning the rules of the road or even the language.

Regardless if you are placing a put or a call, or even just planning your strategy, you must look at your various risks and rewards in terms of three key areas. First, the amount of change the price is likely to experience, second the amount of volatility currently at play, and finally, the amount of time the option has left until it expires. If you are holding a call, you will all need to consider if the price is moving in the wrong direction, if the volatility is decreasing or if there isn't enough time left on the option in question. On the contrary, sellers face the risk of prices moving in the wrong direction and an increase in volatility but never when it comes to the time value.

When options are combined or traded, you will then want to determine the Greeks related to new results, often referred to as the net Greeks. This will allow you to determine the new difference between risk and reward and act appropriately. Understanding what the Greeks can tell you will allow you to better tailor your strategy based on your desired level of risk. You can think of them as guideposts to keep you on the right track when it comes to seeking out the right options for you.

Delta

When dealing with individual options, Delta can be thought of as the overall amount of risk that exists between the price of an underlying stock at the current moment and where it is likely to move. If this is the case, then it means that if the underlying stock moves 1 point, the price of the option will shift .5 points, assuming all other factors remain even. The complete range Delta can be anywhere from -1 to 1. Puts can be anywhere from -1 to 0, and calls can be anywhere from 0 to 1.

Delta is likely the first measurement of risk that you will always want to consider when it comes to choosing the options that are right for you. In this instance, it is beneficial to know the expected results of paying less in exchange for knowing the Delta is going to be lower as well. This difference can be seen by simply looking at the strike price and watching how it changes concerning the put price.

Generally speaking, the cheaper an option is, the smaller its Delta is going to be. It is because delta is often linked to the odds that a specific option is going to be worth a profit by the time it expires. As an example, if you are looking at an option with a Delta of .32, then you can assume, all things being equal, that buying into that option is going to pay out successfully about a third of the time.

Vega

Whenever a position is taken, regardless of what that position is, the risk of change that comes from the volatility of the underlying stock is known as the Vega. The level of volatility that an underlying stock has can change even if the price of the stock in question doesn't. This means that it has the potential to affect their profits significantly. Successful strategies can be built around both low and high volatility choices, as well as neutral volatility choices from time to time.

If the volatility of the option in question goes up in conjunction with its volatility, then that option is said to have long volatility, and if the value increases while the volatility decreases, then it is said to be a short volatility option. Strategies or trades that take advantage of long volatility are said to have a positive Vega, and those that use short volatility are said to have a negative Vega. Options that have a neutral level of volatility can be said to have a neutral Vega as well.

As a general rule, the more time standing between an option and its expiration date, the higher that option's Vega is going to be. This is because time value is proportional to volatility as the longer the timeline, the higher the chance that the volatility will manifest itself. As an example, assume an option is currently worth about $4 with an underlying asset that is worth $90. Further, assume that it has a Vega of .1 with 20 percent volatility. If the volatility increases by just one percent, this will equate to 10 cents worth of increase in the price for a total of $4.10. The amount of change that is seen in an option with a shorter period is often going to result in larger changes because there is ultimately less time the option will restabilize.

Theta

Theta is the measure of the rate at which the time the option has left disappears or decays, which means that this number will often be negative when you are dealing with it. The instant you purchase an option, that option's Theta starts to decrease along with the total value as both decreases the closer the option is to its expiration point. If the Delta of a given option is greater than its Theta, then the option will benefit the holder, and if the Theta is greater than the Delta, then the option will benefit the writer.

As an example, consider an option with a Theta of .015 that is going to decrease in value by 1.5 cents in 24 hours. Puts have negative thetas, and calls have positive thetas. This is because puts are worth the least when they are about to expire, and calls are worth the most because the difference between the starting and ending amounts is going to be at its highest. Additionally, Theta fluctuates day by day as it starts slow and then builds in intensity, the closer the option gets to its last expiration. This explains why long-term options attract buyers, and sellers prefer short-term options.

If you are looking to make a trade when the market is neutral, then you will want to be sure to take Theta into account, but you can otherwise move forward confidently with your current strategy. Generally speaking, you are always going to want to buy into options with a Theta that is as low as you can manage it.

Gamma

If Delta is the amount of change that the option will experience in response to a change in the underlying asset price, then Gamma is the amount you can expect Delta to change over time. Gamma increases as options near the point where the price of the options and the price of the underlying asset overlap and will decrease even further below the strike price as the price of the underlying asset drops.

The larger the Gamma, the larger the risk, but also the larger the return. Gamma is also likely to spike as the option in question reaches its expiration date. It can be taken a step further with the Gamma of the Gamma, which considers the rate the Delta changes.

For example, if a stock is trading at about $50 and a related option is currently going for $2. If it has a delta of .4 as well as a gamma of .1, then, if the stock increases by $1, the delta will see an increase of 10 percent, which the Gamma amount is also. If volatility is low, then gamma is high when the option in question is above its strike price and low when it is below it. Gamma tends to stabilize when volatility is high and decreases when it is low.

Rho

Rho isn't going to come into play as frequently as the other Greeks as interest rates are typically going to increase in tandem with call prices while the price of puts will decrease, and the reverse is true when interest rates decrease.

You can expect the Rho values to reach their peak when the price of the underlying stock crosses the price of the option you are working with. Additionally, this value will always be negative for puts and positives to calls. Rho values are more important when it comes to great options and virtually irrelevant for most short options.

Finding the Greeks

To determine how the Greeks are going to apply to any of the options trades you make, the first thing you will need to keep in mind that every strategy is likely to have a positive or negative value for each of the Greeks.

As an example, if the Vega is positive, then the position will see gains if the volatility rises. Likewise, a negative Delta position will result in a decrease if or when the underlying asset decreases.

Keeping an eye on the Greeks and noting how they change is key to options trading success in both the short and the long term.

To find the Greeks for your chosen option successfully, the first step is always to remember that the results you see are going to be theoretical as no one, and certainly not the Greeks, can predict the future. What you are seeing is just the results of a mathematical formula with several different variables plugged in as needed.

These include the bid you are putting on the option, the asking price, the last price, the volume, and occasionally the interest.

Chapter 12. Call and Put Options

Put and call options are referred to as a derivative investment. The movements of their prices depend on the movements of prices of a different financial product, also referred to as the underlying.

So, what is an option? It is defined as the right to sell or buy a certain stock with a set price given a specific time frame. With options, you won't have outright ownership of the shares, but you make calculated bets on a stock's price and what its value will be in the future, given the specified expiration of the option. What makes options attractive is that you are to choose whether you want to exercise them or not. If your bet is wrong, you can let the options expire. Although the options' original cost is lost, it still wouldn't compare had you paid for the stock's full price.

Call options are purchased when the trader is expecting the underlying's price to go up within a particular time frame. In contrast, put options are purchased when the trader is expecting the underlying's price to go down within a particular time frame.

There's an option for puts and calls to be written or sold. It will still generate income, but certain rights have to be given up to the option's buyer. For options defined for the US, a call is defined as an options contract giving the buyer rights to buy an underlying asset at a set price any time until the expiration date. For options defined for the EU, buyers can choose to exercise the option to purchase the underlying but only on the set expiration date.

The strike price is defined as a determined beforehand at which the call buyer has the choice to purchase the underlying asset. For example, a buyer of a certain stock calls option with a 10$ strike price may opt to purchase that stock at the same price before the expiration date of the option.

The expiration of options may vary. It can also be short or long term. It can be worth the while to call buyers to exercise the option, which is to require the writer or seller of the call to sell the stocks at the set strike price. But only if the underlying's current price is more than the strike price. For example, if a stock trades at $10 at the stock market, it is not profitable for the buyer of the call option to exercise choice to purchase that stock at $11 since they could get the same on the market at a lower price.

Put buyers reserve the right to sell stocks at strike price during a set time range. The highs and lows the stock market goes through can be both exciting and nerve-wracking for newbie or veteran investors. Risking hard-earned money can make anyone anxious. But played right with sound and well-planned strategies, you can be successful in this field

If you are looking for a way to invest in the stock market, but you are trying to avoid the risk of directly selling stocks or buying them, options trading might be perfect for you. Options are typically traded at significantly lower prices compared to the underlying prices of the actual shares. This makes trading them a less risky way to control a long stock position, although you don't own the shares. Using options strategically allows risk mitigation while maintaining huge profit potentials, and you will be playing in the field even if you're investing just a fraction of the stock's price.

All of these benefits of options trading got you excited, right? After all, options have a lower risk, and they're a lot cheaper. There are two major disadvantages, however – the limited-time aspect and the reality that you don't own the stock until you choose to exercise your options.

Call Options

With call options, what you pay for is just 'rights to buy' certain shares at a set price and covered by a specific time frame. Let's say that stock ABC is selling for $90 per share in May. If you believe that the stock's price will go up over a few months, you will purchase a three-month option to buy 100 shares of ABC by August 31 for $100. For this sample call option, you would be paying around $200 if the option cost per share is $2. In options, you are only allowed to buy in increments of 100 shares. This gives you a choice to purchase 100 shares of ABC anytime within the three-month timeframe. The $200 investment is significantly lower than the $9,000 you would have had to shell out if you bought 1000 shares outright.

If you bet right and on July 15, if the ABC shares hit the market at $115, you may exercise the call option, and you would have gained $1,300 (that's 100 shares multiplied by the $15 profit you gained per share and deducted by your original investment of $200). If you don't have the resources to buy the shares, you can also make a profit if you re-sell the option to another investor or via the open market. The gain will be pretty much similar to this option.

If you bet wrong, and the price of ABC's shares fell to $80 never to reach $100 within the three-month timeframe, you can let the option reach its expiration, which saves you money (if you bought the shares outright, your original investment of $9,000 is now down to a value of only $8,000, so you lost $1000). This means you only lost $200, which was your investment for the call option.

Risks Involved in Call Options

Like any other form of investment, options have their share of potential risks. Taking the second scenario where you bet wrong as an example and stock ABC never got to $100 during the option's timeframe of three months, you would have lost the entire $200 of your investment, right? In terms of loss percentage, that's %100. Anyone who's been playing the stock market would tell you that it's extremely rare for an investor to suffer a 100% loss. This scenario can only happen if ABC suddenly went bankrupt, causing the price of their stocks to plummet down to zero value.

Therefore, if you look at it from percentages, options can cause you huge losses. Let's elaborate on this point. If the price of ABC's share went up to $99, and it's the last day for you to exercise the option, choosing to purchase the shares will mean losing a dollar for each share. What if you invested $9,000 for the stock, and you owned 100 stock shares? In three months, which is the option's expiration date, if you took it, you would have gained 10% from your original investment ($99 from $90). Comparing both, you would have gained 10% if you purchased the shares outright and lost %100 if you chose the option but did not exercise it. This example shows how risky options can be.

However, the opposite can happen if stock ABC reached a price higher than $100. If you purchased the option, your gain percentage would have been substantially higher compared to buying the stocks outright. If the stock reached $110, you would have gained 400% ($10 gain versus the $2 per share investment) if you went for the option and only gained 22% ($20 gain versus the $90 per share investment) if you purchased the shares.

Lastly, when you own the stock, nothing can force you to sell. That means if after three months, and stock ABC's price goes down, you can hang on to it if you believe it still has the potential to recover and even increase in value compared to the original. If the price goes up dramatically, you'll make significant gains, and you didn't incur losses. However, if you chose options as your investment method, the expiration would have forced you to suffer a 100% loss after the set timeframe. There will be no option to hold on to the stock even if you believe it will go up in value soon.

Options have major pros and also major cons. You need to be aware of these before you step into the arena of options trading.

Put Options

On the other side of the options, investment is the put option. Whereas call is the right to purchase, 'put' gives you the option to sell a certain security at a set price within a specific time frame. Investors usually purchase put options to protect the price of a stock in case it suddenly drops down, or even the market itself. With put options, you can sell the shares, and your investment portfolio is protected from unexpected market swings. Put options are, therefore, a way to hedge your portfolio or lower its risk.

For example, you have invested in stock ABC for 100 shares, which you bought for $50 per share. As of May 31, the price per share has reached a market high $70. Of course, you'd want to maintain this position in your stock, and at the same time, protect your gained profits in case the price of this stock goes down. To fit your requirements, you may purchase a put option with a three-month expiration and $70 per share strike price.

If ABC's stock price goes down drastically over the next couple of months, reaching a low per-share price of only $60, you will still be protected. By exercising your put option, you will still be able to sell the shares at $70 each, even if stock ABC is now trading at a lower value. If you are feeling confident that ABC can still recover in the future, you can hold on to the stock and just resell the put option. The price of this put option will have gone up because of the diving stock ABC took.

On the other hand, if stock ABC's value kept climbing, just let the put option expire, and you would still profit from the increased price of the shares. Even though you lost what you have invested in the put option, you still have the underlying stock with you. Therefore, you can view the put option as a kind of insurance policy for your investment, which may or may not use. Another thing to remember is that you can purchase put options even if you don't own the underlying stock, just like you would in a call option. You are not required to own the stock itself.

Risks Involved in Put Options

Just as with call options, put options carry the same risks. There is also a 100% loss potential when the underlying stock price goes up, and a huge gain when the price dives because you can resell the option for a higher price.

Chapter 13. Become a Successful Trader

Anyone can become a day trader, but you cannot just immerse yourself in and expect to survive. That is a sure-fire way of wasting the whole wealth in the blink of an eye. If you want to trade for a living, you need to continue with the right mentality and devote significant time and energy to your education.

Characteristics of a Good Day Trader

Anyone can indeed become a day trader, but to survive in the highly competitive market in the long run, you need to adapt yourself according to this business's requirement. You need to develop some qualities that will differentiate you from others, and help you sustain as a day trader. Let's look at some of those characteristics of successful traders:

They Take Full Responsibility

Good traders accept their losses, and they do not dwell on or blame others or conditions. They learn from their failures and carry on their trade. There is a system for successful traders.

They adhere to their system of trade religiously. Many established traders are willing to take responsibility for their success; few are willing to take responsibility for the failure.

There is no talk of the market-maker or broker somehow when they win, the market behaving strangely, the system, their risk management, or mind-affecting their trade.

However, these bugaboos, all of a sudden, appear at the frontline of their thinking during a loss. There is a tendency when things do not go your way, to look at someone other than yourself, the one who pushed the buttons.

Having a responsibility to the gut-level does not distinguish winners from losers. They are identical. In the situation, they all came from the common denominator - you. Will you build up your ego when you excel, or do you draw on what you have done right to do more? Trading holds a mirror to oneself, sees what needs work, and works on it while seeing what works and increasing it. And it is your weakest trading skill that sets the height of your earnings and success. Fortunately, skill is a drill that can easily be molded to build your success's pillars.

They Have a Lot of Patience

Successful traders know most of the positions the minute that they are opened. They have to wait for their moment to come. They are patient enough to handle all the trading uncertainty. Most traders come up with a strategy that helps them decide when and where to enter a trade. That strategy should yield a profit if it is traded correctly. It sounds easy, but traders are facing a problem: when they see a fast-moving chart in real, their mind gets fooled into thinking that you enter a trade before the market structure is fully developed. You are afraid to lose out on a trade, so you enter early and usually end up losing.

Wait for the right setup and trigger your trade ultimately. You also need to be ok with missing an opportunity; take only trades that will give you the right setup and trigger your trade. There should be no trades unless the market causes this.

Have a brainstorming session about what you could do better if you are following your plan and still get into it a bit too early. If the price is higher and begins to go down, consider waiting for that to happen before considering getting in. When the price starts moving sideways, look for small clues that the price is beginning to rise again. If the movement lasts, waiting for the price to go high to cause the trade can help. If the price wiggles around during that pullback, consider watching those tiny price shifts inside the pullback for higher highs and higher lows.

These movements prove the buying pressure will build up again. When the price appears to shift opposite right before it moves in the direction you are expecting, you are waiting for the move to take place and then act. Do not trade until you are sure now is the time to get in. You do not have to capture every big move in prices to make a profit. When you miss a step, then you are missing it.

Be patient; the market takes longer than we would expect to move. By waiting for the right setup and trigger, you will begin to catch more of the price movements you anticipate, and not waste your money on losing trades.

They Have Forward Thinking

Successful day traders cannot get trapped in the past. Although day traders are using past data to help them make trading decisions, they must be able to apply the information in real-time. Traders are also plotting their next moves, deciding what they will do depending on where the market is going.

The markets are not static. We cannot decide in five minutes we are going to buy at a certain amount, and then forget all the market knowledge that is going on in those five minutes. Day traders are preparing their next move always, based on new market information they receive every second. They consider various scenarios that might be carried out and then prepare how they would execute their trading strategy for each of those different conditions.

They do not Overtrade

Overtrading is the unnecessary buying or selling of financial instruments. In many terms, getting too many open positions on a single trade or using a disproportionate amount of capital. There are no laws or regulations for individual traders against overtrading, but this can damage your portfolio. Overtrading can have significant implications for trading brokers, as they are controlled bodies. It is best to avoid overtrading and have a comprehensive trading plan and risk management strategy in place. Stop emotional trading: differentiate between logical and emotional trading decisions and provide sound reasoning for your decisions.

When you already have more than one open position, by spreading your investment through asset groups, you can help reduce risk. Using just what you have: determine how much you want to gamble but never use more money to trade than you can afford to lose. Good traders should not overtrade. They know that overtrading put their account at risk, and not everybody knows it is the day of the trade. They are waiting for an opponent with high probability.

They Are Adaptable

Successful traders are capable of adapting. They customize their trading methods and market-changing decisions. Successful traders understand what kind of dealer they are.

They do not force themselves to trade in methods or strategies; their personality does not fit. You are permitted to make small adjustments to your trading plan after a full month of trading, based on what you learned from your trading plan review sessions. Trades focused on these minor strategic improvements should be exercised for another month and evaluated afterward. Changes should not be made to the plan before the one month, because it is easy to make changes based on individual trades as opposed to overall results.

The issues that come up in your self-review are being worked on every day. For the self-review, all you have to do is follow the trading strategy, whatever it might be. If the trading strategy evolves, so does your company, but it is always your job to follow the strategy. Your daily self-examination does not change the trading plan; instead, you are working on your personality traits to follow the plan. Strive to make minor improvements to the trading strategy weekly. The same concept applies to your day-to-day review of yourself. Work one thing at a time. Trying to solve a lot of problems at once means you are not focusing enough on each problem because your attention is spreading too widely.

They Take Action

Successful traders take action. They do not let them control their fear of their choices or interfere with their business. They use successful systems. Their methods of commercialization and metrics focus on high-probability, sound trades, managing money, keeping its strategies curve free of tying, and incorporating their program in their business plans. It is not enough to just watch videos or read. Day traders need to regularly practice what they are learning before becoming sufficiently determined to be useful in making trade decisions under ever-changing market conditions.

It is not just about putting in hours of action. Day trading is possible for years, putting in hundreds or thousands of hours, and never seeing any progress because you are not focused on a particular activity.

Focus on a particular activity to practice effectively.

Here's where the intention to exchange comes in. A trading plan is a document that specifies precisely how, why, and when a trader joins and exits trades, how they control the risk, and what the size of their position will be. It also specifies which markets are to be traded and when. The practice involves implementing a plan to allow tracking of progress.

Practice day trading in a demo account, one component of the trading plan at a time, until the strategy becomes second nature. You may go through charts, for example, and pick entry points for your strategy. Do this until you see all of the entry points your strategy provides. Day trading requires fast reflexes and accurate timing. Practice so entries occur precisely when they should, depending on the technique. Then move on to putting right the stop-loss. Then practice correctly positioning the target for income. Practice having the perfect size of position on each trade, and every other trading element covered by the trading plan. While it may sound a little strange, you are also learning what not to do this whole time.

Your aim is not only to take action on your strategy and take all the trades you are told to make (when circumstances are favorable, based on your trading plan), but also to practice sitting on your hands when your strategy does not ask you to take a trade. Trading is about the deals you do not carry out as much as it is about those you do. When your plan does not deliver a trade incentive, then do not do it. Most new traders lack the patience needed to wait for a legitimate trade signal, but it can be learned through practice.

Where a legitimate trade opportunity occurs, practice being cautious and pouncing. The amount of time that traders will practice will differ for every item of their trading plan. You will usually work 15 to 20 days on every item of the trading plan. Using this method, a trader should have a clear understanding of their trading plan after about six months, have their strategy practiced for days, and have a reasonable idea of how to use it under all market conditions.

They Are Disciplined

Discipline is a key trait that every trader needs. The market gives you limitless possibilities for trade. Every second of the day, you will exchange thousands of different items, but very few of those seconds provide great commercial opportunities.

If a strategy provides about four to five trades a day and stop loss and goals for each trade are automatically set. During the day, there are just about five seconds of real trading activity.

Chapter 14. Starting on Your First Trade

Starting as a beginner is sometimes a scary thing to work on, and we need to make sure that we are completing it properly. Some of the steps you can take to get started with some of your trades in day trading include:

Decide What Strategy to Use

Some days the market is going to behave in a manner that one strategy will lend itself the best to what you want to do with trading. And then the next day it could be a completely different situation. It is why we need to keep things open and figure out what is going to work the best for our needs here. But when you are ready to do any kind of trading, then we need to go through and pick the strategy that we want to at least start with. We can choose to change this up later on if we would like to. But knowing the strategy that we want to look for, and what signs we need to pay attention to along the way will make a big difference in the amount of success we will be able to use with it.

As a beginner, stick with just one or two strategies and learn them well. You can always wait out the market to see what it is going to do in the future and determine if that is the right course of action for you. If nothing shows up, then you just call that day a wash and don't get into the market.

Pick a Broker

When you are ready to get started with your day trading investment, you need to make sure that you find a good broker. This will ensure that you are going to be able to work with someone who can do the calls and the trades for you. Each broker is going to have different options of stocks that you can use, different tools and methods that you can enjoy, and even can work with different fees that you have to work with.

This is all going to be things that you need to research ahead of time. Each broker is going to be a little bit different from the others, and you need to make sure that you are getting the best deal. Take the time to pick out a broker that has a fee structure that works for you. Some of the fee structures are not going to work all that well if you are doing a ton of trades each day, which is possible with day trading, so we want to look into that and discover whether we like the fee structure and whether it will set us up actually to make us some money.

Decide How Much to Invest

It is always important to know ahead of time we are willing to invest in our trades. You can't just throw in a money based on a "hunch" or how you feel that day, or you will end up losing all of your money and having all of your investing money being gone in just a few seconds.

Before you start with any of the trades that you would like, set aside a certain amount of money that you are willing to lose if things go wrong. You can even go through and work with a separate account that only holds onto the money that you would like to use for investing. If you run out of money in that account, then it is time to stop investing until you have enough money to get started again.

Doing this is going to help us to get started with investing without needing the emotions to show up as well. You have a set amount that you can use, and hopefully, you can earn money in this, but then we also have a good stopping point if we do not see our trades work in the manner that we want.

Look Over the Stocks to Work with

Before you jump into the process of day trading, you need to go through and do some research. There are likely a few stocks that, over time, you are going to get more familiar with and decide the right ones for you to work with. You can go back and forth between them, trading the one that makes the most sense for your needs based on how the market is going at the time. In the beginning, though, you will need to go through the motions and do a lot of research to see which stocks look to be the best for you.

If you have a particular strategy that you want to work with, this can be a great place to start. It will allow you a chance to go through and work on the stocks and look for the ones that are going to fit with this strategy and can help you to get the best results here.

Sometimes you may have a few strategies that we want to work with, and we can look around and see if any stocks are going to match up with these.

There will be a lot of research that comes with this part. We need to be able to look at a lot of charts and graphs and learn about long and short-term trends that come with our stocks, and how we can utilize these for our needs as well. Only when we have a good understanding of the trends that come with the stocks we want to use, then we are ready to enter a trade.

Start Your Trade

When all of the research is done, it is time to start the trade. Work with your broker to set up the trade and do the calls that you want in the market. You can determine the price you want to pay, the volume of the stock that you would like to purchase, and more. Then you can place this order with the broker to get it all done.

Even after placing the order, though, we need to take the time to watch the stocks along the way. Day trading is too fast of a trading option to work with; you can't just set it up and then walk away and call it good. You have to watch it the whole time to figure out whether something is going to happen with the stocks, if the market is working the way that you want, or if there is anything else concerning to watch for.

Put Stop Loss Points in Place

These are going to be critical to ensuring that you are not going to lose too much money if the stock price goes down too much and that you won't end up losing some potential profits by staying in the market too long. And it is a great way to limit the number of emotions that can get into the mix.

Before you start working on a trade, decide how much you would be comfortable with earning on the trade, and how much you would be comfortable with losing.

Then add in stop-loss points into both. When either of these is hit with the price movements, then your trade will end, and you will take the earnings or the lost in the process.

The market can change quickly. You don't want to earn a bunch of profits, and then the market turns and crashes before you have a chance to pull out and take the profits.

You also don't want to get into the situation where your stock takes a freefall, and you are not going to be able to earn anything, and you lose too much because it all goes away in no time. And you will not need to worry about those emotions getting in and cause some issues with staying in the market for too long either.

Get out When Your Goals are Met

While most stocks are going to follow some strong patterns that stick around, but when you are looking at the daily trends, there are a lot of up and down movements. You never know where this volatility is going to head, and having a plan in place is going to be important to ensure that you are set and able actually to make some money.

This topic is where those stop points can come in hand. When you earn the profit that was your goal, you get out. The market can turn in just a few seconds, and it may not get back up. Take any win that you can with this one, and you can always get back in again if you find the market goes back up. Day trading goes too quickly and is too volatile, even with some steady stocks, to mess around and hold out hope that you can make even more. Get out when your goals are met and then work from there.

As you can see, there are a lot of different parts that come together with starting your first trade. It is not always as simple as we would hope, and sometimes we need to go through several steps ahead of time and have a good plan in place to ensure that we are going to see some good trades in a while working with day trading.

Chapter 15. Futures Spread Trading

Many day traders find futures preferable to options because they are sure to always move along with the asset that they are related to. What's more, the futures market can be analyzed directly, which means that you can profit from anticipation on the market without having to take any derivative pricing into account.

Even better, unlike some other markets, no artificial restrictions are limiting your ability to short trade, making your job as a day trader much easier in the process. Finally, this makes it so that FINRA's definition of a pattern day trader does not apply.

A pattern day trader is required to keep $25,000 on hand at all times, among other things, and being labeled as one will make it more difficult for you to trade as effectively as possible.

Always Follow the Trends

Odds are, if you are attracted to futures trading, then you are less naturally inclined to follow trends in the market, preferring instead to jump in on opportunities when they are still forming.

This is a habit that you are going to need to break if you plan on trading in futures, however, as typically you will find that the practice is much more profitable if you stick with the trends of the major players and deviate from them as little as possible.

Don't Prioritize Trade Frequency

While it is natural for day traders to make more trades than other types of traders, that is no reason to assume that there are always future trades that can be made at the moment. It is important to always keep in mind that it is possible to be a successful day trader while making three trades a day just as it is to be successful while making 30 trades per day. It is all about choosing your futures targets carefully and with a clear understanding of where all the trades are likely headed. Don't forget, before you finalize any trade, you should always run a full risk/reward analysis to ensure that it is going to be worth your time in the long run.

Know How a Good Futures Contract Looks Like

Prior to starting any trade, you must take the time to gather as much information as possible to ensure you prevent any further surprises from sneaking up unannounced. First, you must know the contract unit in question as each potential futures contract will show the size as well as the units it is trading in.

Forex futures will always be specified with a given currency. At the same time, those based on stock indices generally include a reference point on the index multiplied by a specific price per share. The specifics of this measurement aren't as important in most instances as they are generally only crucial in the moment to help you understand exactly what you are getting yourself into.

You will need to keep in mind the quoted price as well as how this quote is likely to change between markets. Also, the way they will be written with dollars and cents while other times they will be written with mathematical equations, possibility points or percentages. The result will always work out to be the same, but it is important to know what you are working with before moving forward.

Choosing the Right Contract

Prior to choosing the right contracts to follow, it is important to understand the various levels of insecurity that are taking place in the market in question compared to the potential for a serious payout should things go just right. This is vital as there is a great deal more variance in the futures market than in the others as they encompass a far greater variety overall. When it comes to making these types of decisions, it is also important to remember that past performance is not going to be an accurate predictor of future results in this instance. This means that just because a price has remained stable for several days is no indication that it will continue to do so.

Look for the Right Signals

With day trading futures, it is important to keep in mind that the best results will typically materialize if you use a trio of indicators that don't specifically result in one another. You will need to keep an eye on the sine wave as a means of determining the price when it comes to support and resistance. You have to pay attention to the momentum to determine the volume in comparison to the supply and the pro-am as a means of determining the specific trade size to help determine how much interest the market has in the trade at the moment.

Generally speaking, you can expect to have the ability to plot the sine wave through the lowest chart pane which will give you a measure of the current cycle. When levels of support and resistance are both confirmed you will see the results mapped via dotted lines on the price bars in question. You will also find the momentum plotted underneath the bars indicating the price and it will then be represented by waves to show the volume when it comes to buying and selling.

You will also find various divergence patterns that can then be directly plotted onto various additional price bars as well. When it comes to tracking the pro-am you will be able to easily consider what types of active traders are sitting on various price points. If you find a lot of highs then you can be confident that it means there is lots of position switching taking place at the top of the spectrum. Meanwhile, lots of lows should tell you that the breakout is on its last legs which means it could likely reverse at any time.

Consider the Direction the Trend Is Forming

More so than in more traditional forms of trading, if you manage to find a trend while day trading, then there is a high chance that you will be able to successfully make a profit off of it, assuming it sticks around long enough to let you.

When it comes to confirming the direction of a potential trend, you will want to take note of professionals who are trading in the space before confirming that the trend is set to continue moving forward as well. You will want to keep an eye out for indicators that it has reached a point where its volume is exhausted, as this means it is likely on its last legs.

Stick with a Single Market

While the futures market tends to have various subsections devoted to different markets, this doesn't mean that you should bounce between them all as you will have far more success if you stick to those in which you see some early success. Once you have mastered a specific subsection of the market, you can then move on to the next, but until that point, you will want to focus on the way you can increase success in the long-term.

Futures Spread Trading Pricing and Margins

Spreads

It is vital that you keep in mind that if they are part of a spread, then the individual margins on a given contract will be reduced. For example, if the margin on a given wheat contract alone is $2,000, but if you decide to go short as well as long on wheat in the same year, then the margin between them could potentially be as little as $200. If you go short and long on one commodity split over different years, then the margin will double to $400. The price differential occurs as the volatility of the spread is less than that of the contract in question. Generally speaking, the futures spread gives you the ability to look at the given market movement in slow motion. Thus, if something major happened in the wheat market, then it would affect both contracts, which would provide enough protection against the increased risk that the singular contract doesn't have.

Price Concerns

The price of a specific future spread can be easily determined via the perceived difference in two contracts. To properly determine what the spread's pricing is going to be the easiest way to go about doing so is to simply find the pricing of the spread simply subtracts the month that is being deferred from the price of the front month. If the price of the front-month is the lower of the two, the spread will end up being negative, and if it is higher than the spread will end up being positive. The values for the contracts, as well as the spreads, will remain the same. For example, if the price of wheat is $500 in the first month and $510 the next, then the spread can be said to be -$10, and if it instead dropped to $490, then it would be $10.

Market Types

Contango markets: A market is thought to be contango if the first month is going to have a lower cost than the deferred month. Generally speaking, this means the deferred month is going to cost slightly more than the first month will, thanks to the cost to carry. The cost to carry will take into account the interest rate on the capital that comes along with the operating costs of the location that sells the commodity in question as well as any related storage or insurance costs. This is considered the default state of the market.

Backwardation Markets

A market is said to be amid backwardation if the near months are valued more highly when compared to the months that are the deferred month. Sometimes known as an inverted market, it is the opposite of the standard market condition. This most commonly occurs if the market is in the midst of a bull phase, which tends to be caused by a supply chain issue, often concerning a substantial increase in demand along with an overall limited supply. This type of price differential typically occurs when the front months feel the full brunt of the change, which is then mitigated as the deferred months start arriving. This is frequently the case if the deferred month ends up in the next crop year after the front month.

Regardless of the state of the market at the moment, you must always factor seasonal concerns into all of your choices as well. Generally speaking, you can count on gasoline prices being higher in the summer while prices of coffee, natural gas, and heating oil will be higher in the winter. Furthermore, you must remember all markets will inevitably experience bearish and bullish periods, but those experienced by commodities tend to be far less consistent overall.

Common Spread Types— Commodity Futures

Inter-commodity Futures

These futures involve contracts that are spread across various markets. As an example, if you believe that the wheat market is going to experience a high demand when compared to the corn market then you would buy wheat and sell corn. The specific prices for each don't matter as long as wheat prices beat corn prices.

Chapter 16. Tips for Day Trading Option

As an options trader, there are many different types of assets that you can work with, and even different markets that you can enter. Getting started provides you with a lot of choices to help you earn a profit, no matter which direction the market is heading. Use the following tips to make things easier and to help you become more successful with all of your trades.

Always Be Flexible when Trading Options

When you are working with stocks and some of the other securities out there, you will need to do it on the idea of buying low and selling high. But when you are working with options, this approach often doesn't meet all of your needs.

With options, you can profit even if the market is going down. Options work well no matter what the market conditions are; either there is a lot of volatility, stagnation, downturns, and upturns. As someone new to the idea of trading, you need to think about all of the different options before you.

Always be ready to look at all the various opportunities that are out there, and be prepared to seize them, even in places you may not have considered before. Flexibility is great with this kind of trading because it allows you to see more opportunities and new trading strategies in the process.

Options can be a different game compared to what you may be used to with other forms of trading. If you have been working in the stock market in the past, then you may be unsure about the differences. Make sure that you learn how to trade in options and the differences between stocks and options before you get started with this at all. This ensures that you are ready to take on more opportunities and still earn as many profits as possible.

Use options to hedge and minimize your risk. Hedging is a great technique that you can use as an options trader to help to reduce your exposure and reduce some of your risks. So, let's say that you hold onto a stock from a blue-chip company. You are worried about how the stock may end up going down in value in the following weeks. To avoid this disaster, something that could cost you a lot of money, you would instead choose to do a put option.

This allows you to sell the shares at market price, even if the cost of your stocks ends up dipping. This is an excellent method to use to save your investments and protect your money.

The issue of hedging is such a compelling one that many traders will try out options to keep their investments safe. Remember that there isn't any guarantee, and you may lose out on this for a bit. But the history of options and functional analysis can show that this can help increase your chances of being successful with options.

Working with Break-Even Points

Another thing to consider when it comes to options trading is the break-even points. As a trader, you must understand these break-even points, so you know the best time to get out of a trade, and you don't exit too early and take a loss without even realizing it. The break-even point is often going to be specific, whether it's high or low, that the stock needs to reach before you can start to earn a profit. These break-even points need to also take into account the amount you paid to get into the trade, as well as any fees or costs that you got from your broker to get started.

Figuring out your break-even points can help you to avoid some of the shocks later on, and any surprises that come out then. Many times, traders forget to work with the fees and commissions that they have to pay their broker when it comes to the trades. They will only figure out the break-even part based on how much they originally invested.

Then, when they take the money out at the break-even point, and they have to pay the commissions and fees, they end up losing money in the process — figuring these numbers out ahead of time and take out all of the surprises.

Then figure out any extra fees and commissions that you will owe to the brokers when you are all done. From there, you can determine what the break-even point is to get started. You can then move on from here and figure out the point where you can begin to earn a profit and make your plans on whether this is a good trade or not, based on those calculations.

Always Do Your Research

Before you enter into any trade with options, make sure that you do sufficient amounts of research. Charts are going to be crucial when you work on your technical analysis. But this isn't always enough on its own. When you begin, take some time to figure out what kinds of stocks and underlying assets interest you the most, and then do some further research into those particular assets.

Take your time to learn about the markets that you want to enter. Watch the charts and find out how they work. Learn the history of those assets, and about the companies that own them. Talk to a broker or someone else who works in the market and get their advice.

You will gain a full understanding of the assets, and be better prepared to make the right decisions when it is time to make your trades.

You will find that there are a ton of different sources that you can use to help you do your research, and utilizing as many of them as possible can make a big difference in how well you are going to do with your trades in the long run. Before even entering into the market, make sure that you spend at least a few weeks researching the options and their underlying assets that you are most interested in. The more knowledge that you can add to your arsenal, and the better you understand these underlying assets, the better you will be able to do with your trades.

With that said, you will need to take some time to find the best resources. You will need to find charts so that you can learn the history of the underlying assets. Find several assets that you would like to work with, and bring out as many historical charts as possible. Then move on to other tables about the industry as a whole, and even the whole market, to see where these underlying assets come from. This helps you to get a good idea of whether it is performing under average, at average, or over average, based on how other companies are doing.

You shouldn't stop right there, though. You must make sure that you work with additional resources as well. You need to have information from different online sources (make sure that they are reputable and stay up to date), newspapers, and more.

You need to know what is going on in the market and the industry, and how that is going to affect any of the different assets that you want to trade-in. You never know when a change in the market can make a significant change in how your options, and their underlying asset, are going to behave.

Going with the Flow

As much as possible, you should go with the flow and do a trend with the trend. With options trading, you will often find that the trend is going to be your friend. This can be true in any investment that you choose to go with, and even seasoned traders know that jumping on the trend, especially early on, is an easy way to make some good money in the market. Any time that you are looking at underlying security and trying to assess its worth, never try to make guesses or estimates.

Especially when you are a beginner, these estimates are going to be wrong, and your investing actions are going to be like gambling. But if you trust the trend (which means you have to watch the market and the charts), you will be right most of the time, and you will earn a profit in your trading endeavors.

Your Exit Point or Your Escape Plan

They refuse to let their emotions take charge of their trading goals. Feelings are unreasonable and erratic, while a trading plan is thought-out and logical. As part of your trading plan, you must have a clearly defined exit strategy, one that you stick with no matter what.

To keep this simple, that exit point is the place where you will close out the trade and walk away if the business starts to head south, and you start to lose money.

If you follow this, you can protect your investment, and it ensures that you don't stay in the market for too long. But if you let the emotions take control, you can end up losing a lot of money because you remain in the trade too long.

Before you ever enter into a business, make sure that you list out your exit points.

Know precisely what criteria need to come into play for you to stay in the trade, and which ones you need to follow to leave the business. If you can stick with this, you can limit your losses and ensure that you can make the most profit possible.

Chapter 17. Contrarian Trading

Day traders that use momentum to trade will buy bonds and stocks when their prices are going up and selling them when the prices begin to go down. These people believe that if something is going up in its price, it will continue to do so for a while and that something that is falling will continue to fall. Momentum trading is only one trading strategy, and, for most traders, it works well, especially with a strong bull market.

Contrarian trading, though, is the exact opposite of those momentum traders, and it also can work very well. The belief in the contrarian strategy is that things aren't going to continue to rise forever and that nothing will fall forever.

The contrarian investment style goes against the market trends that are currently prevailing by purchasing assets that are performing poorly, and sell them once they are performing well. This type of investor believes that when another person says that the market is moving up, does so when they are completely invested and aren't planning on purchasing more. This means the market is at its peak, which means a downturn is about to happen, and the contrarian investor has already sold.

A trader that uses the contrarian strategy will look for assets that have been on the rise and will sell them, and they prefer to buy stocks that have been falling in price. It doesn't mean that you should buy cheap or sell but instead look for things that appear to be overpriced and to buy what looks to be a bargain. Contrarian investment also emphasizes out-of-favor securities that have a low P/E ratio.

Breaking Down Contrarian Investing

This investment style is distinguished from others in that they buy and sell against the grain of what other investors believe at a given time. These investors will enter the market when others feel pessimistic about it, and its value is a lot slower than the intrinsic value. When there is such a largely pessimistic view about a stock, the chances of the price lowering so low that the risks and downfalls of the stock are overblown. Finding out which of the distressed stocks to purchase and then sell it after the company has recovered will boost the value of the stock. This is the main play of the contrarian investor. This can even make a security return gains that are a lot higher than usual. But, if you become too optimistic about hyped-up stocks, it can create the opposite effect.

Most investors that use this style see the market as an eternal bear market. Now, that doesn't mean that they keep their view of the market as negative, but instead, they keep a good skepticism as to how different types of investors feel. Overly high valuations will end up causing a drop when an expectation doesn't work out the best. The principles of this kind of investing can be used in individual stocks, an entire industry, or a whole market.

There are similarities between value investing and contrarian investing. They are similar because both types of investors look to identify discrepancies in the price between certain investments, and looking to see if, in the current market, an asset class has been undervalued. Most of the best values investors will see a fine line between contrarian and value investing as both of them look for the undervalued securities to start making a profit-dependent on following the current sentiments of the market.

The biggest difference is the P/E ratio turns important with value investing as opposed to contrarian investing, which considers it but also looks to read the qualitative importance of the overall market. They both also look at trading volume, media commentary, and analyst forecasts.

Contrarians will also look at some of the basic principles that are part of the behavioral finance. Some of the ideas from behavioral finance that they use are that of investors as a whole and how they interact with trends. An example would be that if a stock has performed badly for a while, it will likely stay that way for a while, as well as a strong, secure stock staying strong.

Basics of Contrarian Strategy

The strategy of the contrarian investor isn't as simple as making the opposite decisions of how the public views a stock, or what the trend says. A stock that continues to rise for a long period of time will begin to look good and gain positive sentiment naturally, but that doesn't mean a contrarian investor automatically hates that particular stock. Making choices against a price trend is the toughest way to make a play. This approach is to identify the stocks where the sentiment of the stock is the opposite of what its established trend is. This means that a contrarian investor will look for the stocks that keep rising even though other investors view it pessimistically.

The reason they do this is that the pessimism normally indicates that there are a lot of investors are avoiding that particular stock, and are choosing to sit on the sidelines. If this stock continues to go higher in price, then eventually, this sentiment about the stock will change, and the people on the sideline will start investing, and the money will start to flow in, thereby making the value shoot up in a short time frame. This sort of fast and furious rally is extremely helpful to the investors that are contrarian options traders.

Indicators

To be a contrarian trader, you have to monitor the stock market constantly and read into stocks, which will help you to get a sentiment to feel. You also need to be able to quantify the sentiment, in which you can do this in a few different ways.

Analyst ratings are a fairly straightforward indicator. They will provide you with a buy/hold/sell recommendation for all stocks that depends on what they believe investors need to do. If there is a stock that is rising higher, but has very little or no buy recommendations, then there is a potential for an upgrade, which may end up influencing the people on the sidelines to purchase some of the stock.

Buying put options or shorting a stock are two options for a trader to profit whenever a stock's price starts to fall. This means if you monitor the changes within a short interest and the put buying amount are great ways to quantify stock sentiment, especially negative.

If there are a lot of negative bets that have been placed on a certain stock as it continues to rise higher, the trader that is contrarian is able to assume that there is a lot of sideline money that been added in to continue with the upward trend.

Investors tend to fall prey to short-termism, and they will act upon their emotions instead of using reason. For investors, the pendulum of emotion will constantly swing between greed and fear, and most of the sentiment indicators are supposed to capture emotional extremes.

If anybody would know, he would. He was able to make a killing by buying into the panic that came after the Battle of Waterloo that took place against Napoleon. The quote people credit him with isn't exactly the complete quote Rothschild said. It's believed to actually be, "Buy when there's blood in the streets, even if the blood is your own."

This statement is the heart of contrarian investment, the belief that the worse the market seems, the better chance you have for making a profit.

To help you figure out the sentiment of the market, here are some good indicators:

Trader's reaction – a person's actions speak louder than their words. Indicators that have been based on technical analysis data, opinions, and surveys tend to be subjective. This means you should concentrate on indicators that show the measurable behavior of other investors. You should look at things like Fund Flow, Short Interest, VIX, Put-Call, and other action-oriented metrics.

Fund flow data – the direction that investment dollars flow out and in of mutual funds can give you a perspective of how the masses view it.

Short interest – the more shares that have been shorted, the bigger the pent-up demand there is to buy shares later on.

Strategist Sentiment Indicators

Volatility index – The fear gauge, or VIX indicator calculates all the input from many different calls and put options to come up with an approximate amount of the S&P 500 index that has been implied by its volatility for the following 30 days.

Put-call ratio – this widely used ratio will measure all the trade volume for a bearish put option to bullish call options, and they use it to gauge what the market mood is overall.

Sentiment surveys – some options for this are the Advisors Sentiment Index and the American Association of Individual Investors, and they have weekly surveys that have been conducted by the Investors Intelligence.

Here is an example of a trade made by a contrarian investor:

The stock is Zynga Inc – ZNGA

Zynga negatives:

Between August 2012 to August 2013, stock in Zynga fell by 12%

Experienced some crazy price changes throughout 2013

In late July 2013, it experienced a slide after the company experienced a management shake-up which caused the stock to tumble below what was a 10-day moving average

In August 2013, its equity hit a technical resistance during its 200-day average

Some analysts at Stifel Nicolaus dropped their estimates for Zynga's earnings to show people the company had weakening fundamentals based on how it had performed during the first half of the fiscal year.

Contrarian Positives

But, for a contrarian trader, Zynga proved to be a good stock that they believed would double in the 12 months following August 2013 because it did experience some positive points, like:

In August 2013, they had 65% of the market cap in cash.

The company hired an eight-year Microsoft veteran.

They experienced a Groupon-like turnaround.

Can Contrarian Be Successful? In short, yes, but you have to understand the following three things completely:

- Action and opinion are two completely different things.

- Trends are where you will find the money.

- You need price confirmation for a reversal

To be a successful contrarian trader, you have to realize that action and opinion can and should have a difference. This will lead to different opinions that are related to the sentiment indicator outcome. If investors think the market is on the rise and is about to collapse, they do not need to act on this opinion at the moment. The opinion can be separated from everything that is currently happening. This can give them the chance to profit by trading along with the market, instead of thinking that their opinion needs to be right at the moment. Emotions and opinions can cause lots of problems in trading profitability, especially if a trader begins to develop strong emotions or opinions.

Chapter 18. Majors and Exotics

We are briefly going to discuss the different currency pairs that exist. You can trade the majors, which is what most people are going to be doing—but you can also trade lesser-known and less popular currency pairs. Some of these are known as "exotics." There are advantages and disadvantages to doing so; for example, one issue that should always concern you is the liquidity of a given trading pair. If you are trading the mystery island peso against the secret hilltop dollar, when you need to close your position to exit a trade, it might be hard to find someone to take the other side of the trade to close it out. Of course, there is always the possibility of having the dealer take the other end of the trade, but first, let's take a look at the majors.

The Major Currency Pairs

The U.S. Dollar is involved in some 89% of currency trades, and currency pairs that involved the U.S. Dollar and some other currency from a large, developed economy are called the majors. There are seven major currency pairs. A major currency pair can be any of the following.

EUR/USD

The Euro and U.S. Dollar currency pair is the most popular and widely traded of the majors. The Euro was introduced in 1999, and it's a relatively strong currency that represents all the major countries in Europe that are part of the European Union. Although Brexit is dominating recent headlines, even with Britain as a part of the European Union, it has maintained its currency, the Great British Pound. Hence, the Euro is the currency used by members of the EU on the continent.

When it comes to this currency pair, you are going to want to watch moves by the European Central Bank or ECB, and also the U.S. Federal Reserve. Of course, in any of the majors, you are going to be looking at moves by the U.S. Federal Reserve.

The biggest strength of this currency pair from the perspective of a small retail trader is that it is a highly liquid financial asset that often has substantial volatility. In recent years, the volatility and the magnitude of moves (on average) have decreased somewhat, but it's still a rather strong average pip movement of 200 pips. Since this currency pair is so liquid, getting in and out of trades fast is not going to be an issue. This currency pair is certainly a good choice for beginners, or a trader of any level.

USD/JPY

This is the U.S. Dollar and Japanese Yen currency pair. Japan isn't quite the monolith that it was in the 1980s when everyone thought that Japan would take over the entire world economically. However, Japan still maintains a large and powerful economy dominated by well-known companies like Toyota, Subaru, and Sony, among others. One factor that is important when considering this currency pair is the fact that Japan remains one of the world's largest exporting nations. This means that it's a frequently traded and highly liquid currency because all that exporting means that people have to convert dollars into Yens and vice versa all the time. The interest rate is low, which also makes this currency pair more attractive for holding over longer periods.

GBP/USD

As we mentioned above, despite being a long-time member of the European Union, Great Britain held onto its currency rather than adopt the Euro in 1999. Now that Britain may exit the European Union, for good or for worse, this probably means that the Great British Pound is here to stay for the foreseeable future. Brexit may introduce a lot of volatility in this currency pair, and in fact, in any currency pair involving GBP and so traders may want to pay attention to it at least for the near future. Even after Brexit is finalized, if it ever actually is, then there is likely to be some extra volatility introduced into the price movements of GBP currency pairs. Whether that is in favor of the GBP or against it, it is relevant to the Forex trader. You are not favoring one currency over another because you like it, you are picking currencies based on what works in a given trade.

USD/CHF

CHF is the ticker symbol (to use a stock analogy) for the Swiss Franc. Switzerland is another country maintaining its currency, and given Switzerland's strong banking presence, it's an important currency despite the relatively small size of the country and its economy. Traders consider the Swiss Franc to be an important currency during times of economic trouble, or when there is an international crisis. When there are global problems, in most cases, the Swiss Franc can be expected to increase against the U.S. Dollar because the demand for the Franc rises as people look for a relatively safe place to put their money. So, if there is an economic crisis that you happen to experience, remember this and bet on the Swiss Franc against the dollar. In times of uncertainty, economic downturn, or crisis, the Swiss Franc may also do well against several other currencies such as the Japanese Yen. The USD/CHF pair sometimes goes by the nickname "Swissie."

USD/ CAD

Due to its direct relationship with the United States, the USD/CAD currency pair can be a good trade, even though it doesn't play as large a role in the markets as the EUR/USD currency pair does. When relations between Canada and the United States are good, volatility can decrease for this currency pair. When there are some difficulties, this can lead to increased volatility making it more attractive to trade. Canada has large exports of coal, raw aluminum, iron ore, gold, and copper ore. So to get a feel for how the movement of the Canadian dollar may be trending concerning other currencies, you might want to see if the prices of these commodities are rising or falling. Since Canada is exporting these materials, this generally means that rising commodity prices are good for Canadian currency.

AUD/ USD

Australia is a diverse and highly modern economy, but like Canada, its economic fortunes are often influenced very heavily by the export of natural resources. When it comes to Australia, you will want to pay attention to iron ore and rare earth metals, along with coal. When commodity prices are rising, the fortunes of Australia are often rising with it, but when they are declining, the fortunes of Australia are probably going down as well.

When you are trading any currency pair involving the Australian dollar, you will want to look at the prices of various commodities. Still, especially coal and iron ore, to see how they are going. Australia also exports large amounts of gold, petroleum, and wheat. So favorable pricing moves for these commodities may put the Australian dollar in a position to rise against other currencies.

NZD/USD

The last of the majors is the currency pair between the New Zealand Dollar and the U.S. Dollar. The New Zealand economy isn't as large as the others we've considered, and it's highly dependent on tourism and the export of agricultural products. It is a leading exporter of dairy products as well as lamb and other meats. If dairy prices are rising on commodities markets, this can bode well for any currency pair involving the NZD.

Crosses

If the USD is not in the currency pair, these are called crosses. There are crosses for each of the currencies from major economies, such as the Euro or the Japanese Yen. The majors enjoy the highest trading volume and are therefore the most liquid currency pairs that you can trade, but several crosses also have high trading volume, and so can be good to trade as well.

First, let's look at some of the Euro crosses.

EUR/JPY

As you might imagine, there is a lot of trade that goes on between these two major economies. As a result, this can be a good currency pair to trade. When exports are in favor, Japan might have an edge, in particular when electronic components are considered.

EUR/CHF

This is the Euro and Swiss Franc cross pair. The thing to look for here is the overall economic situation and whether there are any international tensions. Generally speaking, if people are looking for a safe refuge for their money, the Swiss Franc is going to be it. So when times are tough, you might look for increased volatility with this currency pair, and you might also look for the Swiss Franc to be rising in value against the Euro.

EUR/GBP

This is certainly a currency pair to watch with the pending Brexit move, no matter how it turns out. If the situation is viewed favorably in terms of the European Union, then certainly, the Euro is going to rise in value against the Great British Pound. Shortly, at least, the Great British Pound is probably going to be declining in value against several major currencies, although over time, this will probably stabilize. Once things settle down, the Great British Pound is probably going to be rising in value. But for now, look for it to be the weaker member of a currency pair with another major country.

AUD

The Australian dollar is also a good cross to look at when trading with the Japanese Yen, New Zealand Dollar, Euro, Canadian Dollar, and even against the Chinese Yuan. The main thing to look at when it comes to the Australian Dollar is to look at what Australia exports and who is importing from it. When commodity prices are rising, this is something that is going to favor the Australian Dollar against the currencies of those countries that are importing large amounts of raw materials from Australia. China is a big consideration here.

Japanese Yen

Any cross pair involving JPY is going to be important. The key data point for Japan is to remember that Japan has few (if any) natural resources. Still, it's going to be importing a large number of commodities since it has a thriving export business of major manufactured goods like automobiles. Therefore, rising commodity prices may be something that hurts the Japanese currency, while falling commodity prices might help it. This fact means the steel in Toyotas and Nissan cars are going to cost Japanese companies less, and lead to increased sales worldwide.

Exotic Currency Pairs

These are currencies that are not traded nearly as much, but many exotic currencies are going to be associated with developing countries. Examples can include countries like Mexico, Thailand, and Brazil. Some currencies that fall in the exotic category have manipulated or fixed exchange rates, making trading them problematic. The biggest weakness with exotic currencies is that they tend to have small trading volumes. Professional Forex traders are generally not spending their time focusing on exotic currency pairs.

Chapter 19. Strategies for Every Market Condition

There are a lot of different market conditions that you could work with when you end up trading in options. Sometimes the market will rise a little or a lot, sometimes they will stay steady, and sometimes they will fall a little or a lot. And with options trading, you can make money on all of these conditions if you use the right strategy. We are going to spend some time talking about the different strategies that you can use in many different market conditions to help you make a profit no matter what!

Strategies to Use in Every Market

As a beginner, there are a lot of different strategies that are out there that you can keep track of and use the way that you want. But all of this information can be a bit confusing when you first get started. To keep things a bit easier, we are going to take a look at some of the market scenarios that you may run into overtime and how you can pick out the right strategies that will handle these markets and still be successful.

Securities Price Rises a Bit

There are a few options for strategies that are going to work here, including the short put, the bull put spread, and the bull call spread. First is the bull call spread. You can also work with the bull put spread. This one is similar, but you will write the puts on the asset while also buying this amount of puts.

And you can choose to work with a short put. This is simply a sell to open order where you will write the puts on the asset you think will see an increase in price. The best move to do with this one is to write close to the money put options that are going to end up expiring soon. With this strategy, you get the benefit of using simple one, but if the asset ends up going down quite a bit in price, you will lose out on your money as well.

Securities Price Falls a little bit

If something is going on in the market and you think that the price is going to fall a bit, there are going to be three strategies that you can pick as well, including the short call, the bear call spread, and the bear put spread. With the bear put spread, you get the advantage of having a cheaper option compared to just purchasing a put, but the profits are going to see some limitations if the security ends up falling quite a bit, instead of a little.

You can also work with the bear call spread. With this one, you would write outcalls and then purchase calls that have the same asset with the same expiration date, but the ones that you end up purchasing should have a higher strike price. This is an option that is usually saved for some of the more advanced traders because it is difficult, and if your asset falls quite a bit at that time, your profits will be limited. The good news is that if the security doesn't end up moving at all, you will still make a profit.

The short call will be an option that you can choose as well. This is going to consist of the trader writing outcall options at or near the money, using an order that is known as sell to open. Ideally, for this to work, the options should expire soon. With this one, even if your asset doesn't seem to move, you are still able to get a return, but you will lose out if the price goes down quite a bit.

Security Goes up a lot

If you think that your security is going to see a dramatic increase in price soon, there are a few strategies that you can use, including the short bull ratio spread and the long call. The long call is just a buy to open order to purchase calls. The advantage of going with this one is that you do have limitless profits if the price does go up quite a bit on your security. On the other hand, if the security doesn't change in price or if it ends up going down, you have nothing to protect you in this scenario.

The other option to go with is the bull ratio spread, and it is usually another one that will be reserved for traders who have been doing this for a bit. With this kind of strategy, you would need to buy and write calls of the same asset that will expire at the same time. You will be in charge of buying more options that you write. The biggest advantage of this one is that you will have some protection if the asset price does start to fall or doesn't move at all, but it won't provide you with the same profit possibilities as some others.

Security Prices Go Down a lot

If you are working with security and you think that the price is going to go down quite a bit, it is possible to work on a long put, or a short bear ratio spread to help you out. The long put is pretty simple, and it is a good option for beginners. To start with this, you would need to work with your broker to use a buy to open order, and then you would buy a put option on your asset. It is always best to buy at the money contracts, which means that the strike price is going to be the same as the market price. This helps you to keep a better handle on the risk that is going to be involved. If you feel that the security will fall soon, you can pick out a contract that has a close expiration date. The downside to this option is that if the price ends uprising or doesn't move during your time, you will not get the protection you need to cut your losses.

The other option is to choose a short bear ratio spread, and it is a bit more complex. You will buy puts and write puts at the same time, and they will have the same asset and the same expiration date, but you need to make sure that your written puts come in at a higher strike price, and you must purchase more contracts than you end up selling. It helps you get protection if the security ends up staying constant or goes up, though you do end up with fewer profits compared to the other strategy.

Security Rises to a Certain Number

If you have a number in mind that your security will get to and you think that it will reach that place within a certain amount of time, there are a few strategies to work with, including the bull condor spread and the bull butterfly spread.

With the bull butterfly spread, you will conduct three transactions, which is why it is considered more advanced. You will write calls that have the strike price of what you think the asset price will be when it expires. For every two calls that you write, you will need to purchase one call that is the next lowest strike price and then purchase another call that is at the next highest strike price. There can be a lot of profit from this option, but there are no limits to the potential losses.

If you want to get even more complex, you can use the bull condor spread that has four transactions. With this one, you will write calls with each strike price on the lower end of the price range that you want the asset to rise to, while also writing a few calls on the higher end. You can also buy calls at the higher and the lower strike price.

The strategy can be great for profits, but since there are so many transactions in the process, remember that you will have to pay your broker more to complete this.

Security Falls to a Specific Number

For this one, you believe that the asset you will invest in is going to fall to a specific number. The best choice to do with this one is the bear butterfly spread, but there are going to be three transactions that have to occur for it to be effective. You will write the put options at whatever price you think the asset is going to fall to, and then, for every two puts that you end up writing, you are also going to purchase two put options. One of these needs to be a higher strike price, and the other should be lower with them both expiring at the same time. The advantage of doing this one is that you won't end up losing as much money if the asset doesn't move at a price the way that you would like. However, commissions can add up because you are ordering three different transactions.

Security Moves Up or Down at the Price

Sometimes the market may be a little volatile, and you are not sure if it will see a rise or fall in price, but you are fairly certain that it is going to go one way or the other in a big way. There are a few strategies that work well with this one, including the short butterfly spread, long gut, long strangle, and the long straddle depending on what you would like to see happening.

Using a long straddle can be good because you can increase your potential for how much profit you can make; however, if there isn't a big change in your asset, you are going to experience some losses. The long strangle is going to be cheaper than the other option, but you do need to see a larger change in the asset price for it to do you any good.

You can also choose to work with the long gut if you are a beginner because it will involve buying in the money call options while also purchasing in the money put options. All the things that you purchase should end up with the same expiration date, and you should end up with the same amount of call and put options when you are done. If you think that the asset will move soon, you want to pick out options that have a short expiration date.

There will be three separate transactions for this one, including selling in the money calls, selling the same amount of out of the money calls, and buying twice as many at the money calls. All of these options need to end up with the same expiration date. For the strike prices, you're out of the money calls should end up proportional to the amount that your money calls at in the money. If you are with a strike price that is pretty close to the asset price, the asset won't need to see much movement for you to see a profit, but the profit will be smaller.

Chapter 20. Trading the SPX and SPY

An Introduction to the SPX

This index consists of the stocks or shares of 500 top American companies with Large-Cap. The S&P 500 stock market index belongs to Standard & Poor's, abbreviated as S&P, and it is a division of the giant McGraw-Hill company.

All the stocks in the S&P index are traded on the two largest stock markets in the USA. These are the New York Stock Exchange and the NASDAQ. The most widely tracked indices of US stocks are the Dow Jones Industrial Average and the S&P 500. The S&P 500 ratio to as the SPX or INX.

There are plenty of exchange-traded funds and index funds that regularly track the daily performance of the SPX or S&P 500. These funds hold stocks similar to those held by this index in the same proportions. The aim is to match its performance on the stock market but before expenses and fees.

These funds choose to align their investment plans with the SPX index because any corporation that has its stock added to the list is likely to perform better at the bourse.

The principal will, in return, boost the performance of the fund as fund managers will most likely buy the shares of companies that get onto the list. The S&P 500 is also used often as a baseline level where the performance of mutual funds and asset management companies is gauged.

Trading the S&P Index with Leverage

There are various ways of trading options with the S&P 500 index or the SPX. You can trade the SPX Index with some built-in leverage in various ways. These are listed below.

Trading the SPX Index option itself: with this option, you have zero leverage. This particular trade with the SPX index is not too common because the index is very large, and the options are very costly. The bid-ask spread is also very wide.

SPY ETF or Great ETF: With this type, the index here is .01 the size of the SPX. There is excellent liquidity with a $0.01 spread. Here, there is no leverage, too, and you need to buy huge amounts of shares.

SSO and SDS: Here, you get double the leverage of the SPY, which is great. This option provides you with great liquidity, which is also another attractive feature. And with a $0.05 bid-ask spread, it is an acceptable option.

There are a few more recently added instruments that you can use with the SPX Index. These additional instruments are the SPXL and the SPXS. The former, as the name suggests, is a long instrument with three times the leverage of the SPX. The latter is a shorter version but also has the same 3X leverage.

Trading Options based on the S&P 500

The S&P 500 index options can be defined as options contracts that are based on stocks whose underlying value is related to the levels of the S&P 500 index. This index is also known as the SPX.

This index is a capitalization-weighted index of some 500 regularly traded, large-cap stocks in the USA. The SPX index options contracts whose underlying value is equal to the total value of the S&P 500 index. It trades with the symbol SPX, and its contract multiplier has a value of $100. The SPX options index is also a European-style option, which means it should be exercised on the last business day just before it expires.

Small-sized contracts and retail investors are all eligible to trade in SPX index contracts. There are mini-sized contracts available to them known as mini-SPX. The index for the mini-SPX is the XPS. It has its underlying value, which is scaled down greatly to the tune of 0.1% of the S&P 500 index. However, the multiplier is still the same, pegged at $100. Here are some examples of mini-sized options contracts.

Option Product >> symbol >> underlying value   >> contract multiplier >> style

S&P 500 >> SPX >> full value >> $100 >> European

Mini-SPX >> XSP >> 0.1 of S&P 500 >> $100 >> European

How to Trade SPX Options

As a trader or investor, you can profit from a rise in the value of the S&P 500 if you are bullish. To profit, you need to buy SPX call options. However, if you think that the index will fall in value, and then you should purchase SPX put options. It can be an example shown below.

Let us assume that the S&P 500 index is trading at 815.94. Now the value of the SPX is based solely on the exact value of the underlying S&P 500 index. This means that the SPX value is also 815.94. This option has a nearby strike price of $820, priced at $54.40. You should remember that the contract multiplier is $100 so the total premium payment that you need to make to purchase the call option is

$54.40 * $100 = $5,440.

When the option eventually expires, the value of the S&P 500 index has gone up by 15% and is now valued at 938.33 points. This increase corresponds to the increase in the value of the SPX, which is also now at 938.33 points. Since this figure is now significantly higher compared to the option strike price, the call options you invested in have now come into the money. If you now choose to exercise your option, you will get your profit, and the amount will be derived using the formula indicated below.

Cash amount = (index settlement value – strike price) * contract multiplier

The cash amount will be (938.33 – 820.00) * 100, which gives the amount of $11,833.10. Remember that the initial investment was $5440, which was paid out to buy the call option. The net profit, therefore, will be;

$11,833.10 - $5,440.00 = $6393

In reality, though, you will not have to exercise the index call option to realize the profits. All you need to do is to close out your position by disposing of the SPX call option at the options market. The profits that you receive from the sale will be inclusive of the remaining time value should there still is time left on the option before expiry.

If you note in the above example, the trade was exercised on the expiration day, so there was no time value benefit to cash in on. Therefore, the total amount received was equal to the SPX intrinsic value.

Limited Downward Risk

There are some advantages of riding the long SPX call strategy. One of these is the fact that the total possible loss that you can incur is exactly equal to the money paid to buy the SPX call option.

For instance, assume that the S&P 500 index fell by 0.15 instead of rising. This would push the SPX value down to the amount 693.55. This value is significantly lower than the option strike price, which is 820.

If this situation plays out, then there will be no need to exercise the call option simply because it would result in a loss. However, because this is an option contract and not a futures contract, there is no obligation to do anything anyway. Letting the contract expire would be the wise thing to do because the options are worthless. The total loss that would be incurred is the cost of the call option, which was $5,440.

More about SPX Options

Whenever you are using options to invest in the S&P 500 index, there are two tools that you can use. These are the SPX and SPY. Both are options that are readily available to traders and investors. These options are considered ideal because they are easy to get in and exit any given position. They are also loved because of their high liquidity nature when trading volumes are high.

We have already learned that the SPX is the Standard & Poor's 500 Index and is incidentally the stock index that is based on the 500 largest companies trading on the NASDAQ or NYSE. These companies on the S&P 500 index are largely based on the market capitalization. Market capitalization refers to the total number of outstanding shares * stock price.

The Dow Jones Industrial Average is indexed that is composed of an equal number of shares of 30 companies, while the S&P 500 is a capitalization-weighted index. In this index, the weight of a company is the result of its market capitalization of a company divided by the total market capitalization of the total number of companies contained in the index.

Underlying Assets

With the SPX options, the underlying assets do not trade, and there are no shares to trade. Provides SPX is a general index, and its price is calculated just like it was a real portfolio with all the shares of each of the companies listed therein. This is why the lists of the 500 stocks are updated regularly.

The SPY

As opposed to the SPX, the SPY is an ETF or exchange-traded fund. SPY is also referred to as spiders. The market price of the SPY is usually determined by an auction market, just like that of other securities. When investment managers build portfolios, they sometimes try to imitate the yield performance and price of the S&P 500 Index.

Such portfolios, based on the SPY, just managed to mimic the performance of the SPX index approximately. However, the results are, in most cases, acceptable and seem to satisfy all the people who trade in the related shares. With SPY, investors receive quarterly. The importance of this is that call options that are in-the-money are regularly exercised to allow the traders to collect their profits.

Major Differences Between SPX and SPY

The SPY pays out a dividend to investors, but SPX does not. Dividends are often paid out on the 3rd Friday of March, June, September, and December. These dates correspond with the options expiration days.

SPX options are European style options and are only exercised at the expiration date. This is as opposed to SPY options, which are American style and can be exercised at any time once the trader purchases them.

While SPY options are settled in terms of shares, SPX options are often settled in terms of cash. Typically, the ITM value that an option has will be transferred from an options seller's account directly to the account of the option buyer or owner.

The value of one single SPX option is equal to 10 times the value of one SPY option. The ratio is usually 1:0.1. This is a crucial factor, and traders need to keep it in mind.

SPY trades approximately $120 while SPX trades at $1200. One money call option on SPX buys $120,000 worth of securities. Similarly, one SPY money call option gives the owner the right to purchase $12,000 worth of securities. If you are a trader and deal in plenty of options all at once, then you would be better off trading the 5 SPX options rather than 50 SPY options.

Chapter 21. Options Trading

In this, our main aim is to equip you with the skills that will help you start as an options day trader. Let's get started.

What Are Options?

An option is an agreement that comes in the form of a contract that allows a trader to buy or sell a financial asset at a specified price over some time. If that wasn't clear, don't worry, we have plenty of time for me to explain it to you. For now, all you should keep in mind is that options are agreements. There two types of options, call options, and put options. Call options are an agreement to buy a financial asset during a certain period at a predetermined price; this price is called the strike rate. Put options are an agreement to sell a financial asset at a strike price within a certain period. The amount paid for an option is called the premium.

Here are some examples of what an option might look like. Options agreements are often of 100 shares. So, an investor might buy an option of company X's stock at $27, which expires on the third Friday of that month. This is the normal day that options expire in the US. The money they paid for the option gives them the ability to sell or buy the underlying stock at a certain price. They don't own the stock. So this investor will have paid for a contract to do something with the underlying asset before the expiry date.

Suppose you are curious as to why someone would do this. It is normal to be. For now, we have learned three things:

- Options are contracts or agreements.

- Options have a time limit, an expiration date.

- Options grant their owner the ability to buy or sell the underlying stock, but they don't own that stock. All they have is permission.

Call Options

A call option is an agreement to buy a stock, generally 100 shares, at a strike price. The person who sells options is called the writer. He sets the price for the option, which is called the premium; the writer is usually the one who owns the stock. The writer of the stock takes into consideration the current value of the stock, time left, and other factors to determine the premium. The writer sells options so that he can collect extra income on a stock he owns and for other reasons like tax management. He is hoping that the call option will expire worthlessly, so he will not lose any money from issuing the option but collect the premium anyway. Let's turn to a more vivid example.

John owns two hundred shares of the Lemonade Stand. His shares are worth $1 each, and he wants some extra income on his shares. So he writes a call option for a hundred of his shares at $0.20 with a strike price of $1.10 until the third Friday of the month. $0.20 x 100 is $20, so John will collect a $20 premium. John has agreed with the person who bought the call option that he will sell his shares at $110 when the person buys it. John is hoping that the price of his stock will not rise above $110 because if it does, he will lose money, and the person who bought the call will be buying shares from him at a discount. That person can then sell those shares back at a higher price, making a profit. This agreement stands until the expiration date. If Lemonade Stock stays below $110, John will keep the $20 at no cost to him.

Mark is the one who wishes to purchase the option. Unlike John, he believes the price of John's stock will increase above $110. So he buys John's call option at $20. Then he watches day after day how John's stock performs. If the price of his stock plummets, Mark will not exercise his call option. He should buy the stock at the current market price than the price in the contract. Now, assume the price jumps to $1.20 per share, which is $120. Mark would be in the advantageous position of buying a hundred shares at $110, and John would have to sell them to him at that price. Mark would then sell the stock on the market or back to John at the current market price, which is $120.

As you have noticed, Mark still hasn't made a profit, he spent $20 for the call option, and he only got $10 in return. So the price has to change enough that exercising the order makes you a profit after all fees have been considered.

Let's go through it again. Mark bought a call option at $20. The option allows Mark to buy a hundred shares of Lemonade Inc. at $110 at any time before the expiry date. Two weeks later, the single share price of Lemonade Inc. trades at $1.20 per share, which costs $120 per hundred shares. Mark exercises his call order and buys a hundred shares valued at $120 at the agreed amount of $110. It is a discount! Mark sells those same shares at the market price, which is $120. On that transaction, he makes $10, but considering he paid $20 for the privilege, Mark has lost $10. If Mark had paid $10 for the call option, he would have broken even. If the price had risen by more than the premium he paid for the call option, he would have made a profit.

If the price of Lemonade Inc. stock rises above $110 after the expiration date, the contract does not apply. This means Mark cannot buy the 100 shares at the strike price, and he will have to pay the same price as everyone else on the stock market. People like Mark are bullish traders. They believe that the price will go up. Of course, real-life call options don't cost as much, but they are similar in every way I have shown here.

Put Options

Put options are an agreement to sell an asset at a set price, the strike price, within a specific timeframe. The other way to think of put options is to think of them as insurance. Let's say you pay $150 a month for your car insurance. Your insurance provider collects a premium, $150, from you. Most of the time, nothing happens, they take your money and get to keep it. The agreement is if you incur damages, your insurance will pay for it. That is what the premium is for.

Your Lemonade Inc. shares are the car, and the put option is the insurance. You pay a premium to them so that if your stock plummets past a certain price, they will buy your shares from you at the strike price. Let's say your Lemonade Inc. shares are worth $1,000 combined, at $10 a share. Then you buy a put option at a premium of $30, $0.30 a share, at the strike price of $9.90 per share. In the event the share price falls below $9.90, like $9.80, the issuer of the put option will have to buy the shares at $9.90 per share instead of the market price. Then you can buy it back from them if you want to short the stock, effectively selling high and buying low. If you are confident that the market price will continue to dip, you can continue to hold off on exercising your put option until you feel confident that you will make the most money.

If the price dips below your share strike price after the expiry date, you cannot exercise your put option. It only applies within the set time frame.

It's worth taking a moment to look at the things we have learned so far before moving forward:

- The amount paid for the call and put options is called a premium.

- A call options contract only reflects an agreement, not ownership of the underlying asset.

- The strike price is agreed upon by both parties as the price to sell or buy at.

- An option holder can exercise an option anytime they want except after the expiration date.

In-the-Money

In-the-money is one of those terms you will often hear in trading. Here we will take a look at what it means as it relates to options. A call option is in-the-money if the option holder is in a position to buy the underlying asset at a price that is below the market price. A put option is in-the-money if the option holder can sell the underlying asset at a price above the current market price. What this name suggests is that there is a value to the option as it is. But this does not mean that exercising the options will lead to a profit. The profit of an in-the-money option heavily depends on whether there is money left over after you deduct fees and commissions. There is still a need for the price of the underlying asset to move further, enough so that the trader realizes a profit. Some options are already in-the-money when you purchase them. The problem with buying them is that they are expensive and the price will have to move more until you make a profit.

Imagine that there is a call option for Lemonade Inc. that is in-the-money at $40 a share, while the stock currently trades at $43. It looks like good positions because it would allow you to buy a hundred shares valued at $43 for the low price of $40. Like this: buy a hundred shares at $4,000, then sell them at $43 and get $4,300, making a profit of $300. But imagine if the premium for the contract were $4 a share, you would not make a profit. Instead, you would lose $100 like this: after selling your shares, you will have $300 as a profit. Then you deduct the premium of $400 from the amount, which will leave you with a negative $100. So if a call option is in-the-money, it does not mean you are guaranteed to make a profit, it only means that the underlying asset is selling above the strike price.

Out-of-the-Money

Conversely, a call option is out-of-the-money if the strike price is higher than the market price. A put option is out-of-the-money if the underlying asset if selling below the strike price. An out-of-money call or put option will be cheaper than a call or in-the-money put option. Once you have bought it, the option may change to in-the-money as the price of the underlying asset fluctuates.

Imagine Lemonade Inc. stock is selling at $40 a share when you buy put options with a strike price of $37. This means you will sell a hundred shares below their market place value, losing $3 per share. But as the price fluctuates, the same put option may be in-the-money if the market price drops to $33. Suddenly you will sell your hundred shares $4 above the market price. Meaning you stand a chance to make $400 by shorting.

Chapter 22. The Benefits of Options Trading

We're not the only ones who believe there are substantial benefits in options trading. The Options Industry Council compiled data to analyze just how popular options trading had become. In 1999, the total number of options contracts traded on U.S. exchanges was a mere 507 million. Although this figure sounds impressive, compared to today's ever-increasing options traders, it attracted a fairly conservative number of investors.

Options trading was soon to be discovered as a great way to make higher profits, though. In 2007, the number of options traders had grown to a whopping 3 billion. Since that time, traders have continued to enjoy all the benefits of options trading, but they've had to be willing to assume the losses as well.

It also attracts investors that have adapted to those changes quite successfully and have found ways to use options trading to hedge their stock equity investments as well. Options trading isn't the only tool in their portfolio, but it provides additional opportunities like no other.

As exciting as owning stock can be, options trading brought with it a much broader scope. Now, instead of holding a small number of shares that reached the boundaries of their financial capital, investors were able, for the first time, to extend the boundaries. When options trading became the norm, investors could now control a much larger number of shares with far less invested capital. They could expand their book, open their portfolios to encompass more diverse holdings, and take advantage of all the flexibility options trading offered.

To many investors, options trading must have seemed like going to Disneyland. All these choices, types, styles, opportunities—I guess that's why they call it "options." What some found, though, was with greater opportunities to profit also comes more ways to experience loss. Now the trader didn't have just to worry about whether his stock would increase, but he could benefit by predicted whether it would go up or down within a certain amount of time.

What a new concept! Your stock didn't have to increase for you to make money; it just had to move—or did it? Not in today's options market. You can even buy options based on a stable, non-fluctuating market. Suddenly there was an alternative school of thought, and the intrigue has enticed investors ever since.

There are many benefits to using some of the key features of options trading. So, let's identify and explain these features and benefits.

Protection

During times when the market is volatile, protective put options can hedge a long stock position against a sharp drop in the underlying stock price. Think of it as the way a life insurance policy protects your family. You are not planning on dying, but should it come to that, your family would be able to survive.

Let me use another example regarding hedging as it relates to options trading. Let's say you decide to invest in seatbelt manufacturing. A company by the name of Keepsafe is rolling out a revolutionary seatbelt that you think is going to change the industry significantly. Keepsafe's seatbelts are being touted as twice as strong and capable as their competitor, loose fit. For this reason, you feel Keepsafe's share value will show an increase this next year.

However, since you're a wise investor who has planned and investigated the industry, you also realize that seatbelts, in general, are subject to a lot of government regulations and safety approvals, which might make this stock rather volatile. This is known as industry risk. What happens next? Well, you'll need to find a way to reduce this risk. You can hedge by going long on Keepsafe and short with a loose fit. Let's pretend the value of the shares for each company will be $1,000.

Here's how it works. If the whole industry goes up, you will make a profit on Keepsafe, but you'll lose some on a loose fit. If the entire industry tanks, you will lose money on Keepsafe, but you stand to profit on Loose fit. Sure, your overall profit that could have been made by not hedging is minimized, but you didn't have as much industry risk. You can hedge a long position with put options, or a short seller can hedge a position through call options.

Volatility Trading

There are so many ways an options trader can invest, and one of those is to predict whether there will be movement or no movement in the underlying stock price. This is what volatility trading is all about, allowing the trader to profit no matter the direction of the market.

Leverage

Being about to leverage is one of the greatest benefits of options trading; the investor controls the same amount of equity with only a small fraction of the capital needed.

Unlike other investments where the risks have no boundaries, options trading are still going to take risks, but they are more defined. Option buyers cannot lose more than the price of the option, or the premium. Most of the time, options are based on equity shares of an underlying investment. Other underlying investments on which you can place an option include Exchange Traded Funds (ETF's), foreign currencies, or commodities like industrial products or agriculture, government securities, or stock indexes.

When leveraging, investors fix the price for a particular period to allow the sale of 100 shares of an equity for a premium price, which is only a percentage of what it would cost if the investor had to pay to own the equity. Remember, the option is only trading risks. When you leverage, you increase your investment power while increasing the possibilities of greater rewards from equity's price movements, or ticks.

When you discuss the benefits of options trading, you cannot avoid speaking about how you can protect and leverage the equity of a volatile underlying stock price. You also cannot help talking about the cost efficiency of options trading.

Cost Efficiency and Practicality

Here's another example of how options trading offers practicality and cost-efficiency. It just makes more practical sense to buy options that will give you the same equity power without the enormous upfront cash outlay. For example, if you wanted to buy 200 shares of Chico Goods while they are trading at $131 a share, you would have to take $26,200 out of your account. Instead, you could have turned to the options market, picked up an option that closely mimics the stock, and bought a call option with a strike price of $100 for $34.

Buying two contracts would give you a size equivalent to the 200 shares of Chico Goods, but your total investment would be $6,800 instead of $26,200 with Chico Goods equity position. Because you still have so much more money in

163

your account, you can use it just to gain interest or apply it to another investment opportunity and diversify.

If Used Properly, Options Can Be Less Risky

The most obvious reason that options can be less risky is that they don't require as much upfront money.

With just a fraction of the cost, investors can control the same value of equity shares. As we've already mentioned, options are the most reliable form of a hedge. Another great benefit of options is that the options market does not shut down at market closing. They protect you 24/7, and that is one of the main reasons they are considered more dependable for hedging.

A word of warning, though, options trading can only be less risky if the investor knows how to use them properly. It may take a few losses under your belt for you to figure out how and when to buy options. If you are short on capital, options may not be for you.

Then again, it may not be for you to invest in a stock of any kind if you don't have the backing to see you through some losses.

Options Offer more Alternatives

Options traders learn multiple ways to achieve their same investment goals. You can trade based on the decrease or increase in stock value. You can trade based on movement or no movement of the stock price.

You can trade based on the passage of time and volatility of the market. Play your options right, and you could potentially profit in every kind of market. Brokers see the

164

upswing in options trading, and because of this is also being more flexible with their fees, making it more feasible for investors to buy multiple contracts and take multiple positions in each one.

Chapter 23. Step-By-Step to a Successful Trade

Usually, the US stocks have over 8,000 stocks on the list, but a typical day trader has access to only a fraction of them because they just fail to build a fortune due to lack of an effective trade strategy. They enter the market based on rumors and exit it empty-handed as a result. More often, they play at the cost of their precious capital. Winning can be hard in the stock market if you lack discipline as a trader. You need to identify the right stocks to create a winning situation for you. Despite the presence of the learning curve, the effort to detect the right stock is worthwhile.

Building a Watchlist

There is a visible difference between a watchlist and a portfolio. Before you head off to a start, you should know that a portfolio is a collection of the stocks you own at a given time while a watchlist displays the securities that you own and also the ones that you have selected even if you don't have any investment in them. Watchlists give you insights into the stocks that you will eventually want to add to your personalized portfolio.

You should create watchlists based on some current factors. You also need to use your previous watchlists if there are any. They would remind you of the searches that you have done in the past and would also help you fine-tune your future searches. Go through the list more often and also plan a personal schedule of how you will be able to comb through the list and see if the stock matches your criteria. In case of negative signals, delete the stock and save your time to focus on other stocks on your watchlist.

Start with the broader sets and then narrow down your stocks while you tailor them down as per your needs. If you know about your requirements, you can weed out the stocks that don't fulfill them. The key is to keep the list up to date. As the stock market reinvents itself each day each hour, you ought to reinvent your watchlist in the same way.

It is the best strategy to keep an eye on the stocks that seem to be popular. Keep an eye on the upward and downward trends in the popular stocks. When you keep an eye on the rise and fall of certain stocks, you will be able to trim and tune your watchlist. You will no longer need to enter the stocks of only the big companies. Instead, you can prepare your watchlist for small companies.

While you prepare a watchlist, you should keep an eye on the candlesticks, dojis, and charts. The fluctuation of prices is another element to watch for. You can build an effective watchlist by collecting liquidity components in the stocks, adding scanned stock listings that meet general technical criteria. Rescanning the watchlist to see which stock is ripe for investment and which should be discarded from the list after a while is also the key strategy to add to your skillset.

For example, you can say that if a stock's volume has been unattractive for the past few days, the stock should be off of your watchlist. Deletion is necessary to unburden a watchlist. The shorter it is, the more you will be able to keep it into consideration.

Introduction to Candlesticks

Candlestick charts came into use after 1850. The credit for the development and use of these candlestick charts goes to Homma, who was a trader from a town named Sakata in

Japan. It is believed that his original ideas were gradually modified as well as refined over several years of trading. To create and study a candlestick chart, you ought to have a data set that contains the open, low, high, and close values for a particular period that you want to display in the chart.

The hollow portion of a candlestick is labeled as the body of the candlestick. Some also call it the real body. The long thin lines in the candlestick that are above and below the candlestick are labeled as shadows. These are also referred to as tails or wicks. These are high and low ranges.

The high is the top of the upper shadow, while the low is the bottom of the lower shadow. If the stock is closing higher than the opening price, a hollow candlestick will be drawn with the bottom of its body, showing the opening price, and the top showing the closing price. If it closes lower than the opening price, there will be a filled candlestick with the top of its body showing the opening price and the bottom showing the closing price.

As compared to bar charts, a majority of traders prefer candlestick charts because they are appealing and also easier to interpret. Each candlestick represents a price action. Hollow candlesticks with a greater close than the open allude to buying pressure while filled candlesticks with a greater open than the close allude to selling pressure.

In this picture, the two candlesticks with dots below them can be taken as examples of hollow and filled candlesticks.

Long vs. Short

The long body candlestick shows intensified buying or selling pressures on a stock or a currency. On the contrary, shorter candlesticks allude to little price changes. They also represent the consolidation of the price. Long hollow candlesticks that you can see in the chart show buying pressure. The longer it is, the higher the stock or currency will close above the opening price. This shows that the price moves fast from the opening level to close and that buyers had been aggressive. Long hollow candlesticks show that the stocks are likely to remain bullish. After an extended period of declines in the prices, the long hollow candlesticks mark a support level.

Long black candlesticks show powerful selling pressure. The longer it is, the further it will be below the opening price. This shows that the prices significantly dropped from the opening position and that the sellers had been aggressive. After a long period of advance in the prices of a stock or currency, a long black candlestick can herald a resistance level. After a long drop in prices, a long black candlestick indicates panic selling.

Marubozu

More powerful are the Marubozu brothers that usually are in white and black. Marubozu doesn't have upper and lower shadows. A white Marubozu is formed when the opening price is equal to the low price, and the closing price equals the high price. This shows that buyers are in control of the price action right from the first trade to the last one. A black Marubozu is formed when the opening price stands equal to the high price, and the closing price stands equal to the low price. This shows that sellers are in control of the price action right from the first trade to the last trade.

Long vs. Short Shadows

The upper shadows of a candlestick show the highest point of a session while a lower shadow shows the lowest point of a session. Candlesticks that have shorter shadows shows that most of the trading action stayed confined near the open and close prices. Longer shadows indicate an extension in the opening and closing prices.

Candlesticks that have a longer upper shadow and shorter lower shadow allude to the fact that buyers were in domination and that they bid prices higher, but ultimately sellers pulled the prices down. This contrast and high and low close created a long upper shadow. On the contrary, candlesticks that have a longer lower shadow and a shorter upper shadow will indicate that sellers dominated in the session and that they drove the prices to the bottom. It also indicates that buyers resurfaced, later on, to bid higher prices at the end of a session.

Spinning Tops

Candlesticks that have a long upper shadow and an equally long lower shadow with a small body are labeled as spinning tops. Spinning tops indicate a state of indecision in the markets. The real body, whether it is hollow or filled, represents little movement in the price from open to close. The upper and lower shadows show that both bears and bulls had been active in the last session and that neither of them could gain the upper hand in the market. A spinning top shows a kind of standoff between buyers and sellers.

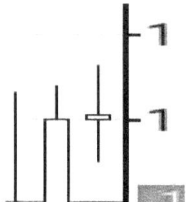

Example of a spinning top

Doji

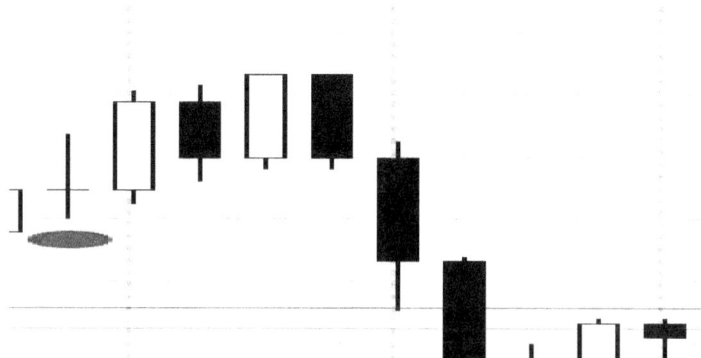

A doji represents a very important type of candlesticks. It offers plenty of information on their own as well as by forming patterns—doji form when the opening and closing points of security virtually stand equal. In a Doji, the upper and lower shadow can vary in length, and the resulting doji looks like a cross, a plus sign, or inverted crosses.

The open-close ought to be equal in an ideal state. This type of doji is considered robust. A doji indicates a tug of war between bulls and bears. Prices move up and down the opening level during a session, and no one can gain control over the market. A doji that is formed among other candlesticks that have long bodies deemed more significant.

The relevance of a doji depends on its preceding candlesticks. After a long hollow candlestick, a doji indicates that buying pressure will weaken. After a fall in prices or a long black candlestick, a doji signals that selling pressure will start to diminish. Doji alone cannot mark an advance or reversal in the price.

After a long hollow candlestick, a doji points to a decreasing buying pressure. If there is a long black candlestick with a decline below the opening price after the doji, this alludes to bearish confirmation in the market. Therefore, after a long hollow candlestick, you should look out for an evening doji star.

If a doji comes after a long black candlestick, it shows selling pressure is diminishing and that the downward trend nears its end. A long hollow candlestick after that shows bullish confirmation, so as a trader, you should look out for this pattern, which is commonly known as a potential morning doji star.

A long-legged doji has equal upper and lower halved. They represent indecision in the market. It indicates that the prices are trading above and below the opening level.

A dragonfly doji forms when the open, close, and high are equal, with the low creating a lower shadow. The candlestick will look like a T as there will be a shorter upper half. A dragonfly indicates that sellers are dominating the market and that the prices are dropping, but by the end of the session, the prices will circle back to the opening level. Gravestone doji is formed when the opening, lower, and closing prices are equal, and the high will create a long upper shadow on the chart.

Chapter 24. The Rules of Day Trading

Let us turn our focus to some of the rules of day trading that every investor should follow. These rules are not necessarily set in stone. You can decide to take these rules with you on your investing journey or ignore them. However, they should be followed to give you the best day trading experience from the very first day of your investing career.

Day Trading is a Serious Business

When some people start day trading, they think that it is meant to be fun and games and do not take the profession seriously. This can be a grave mistake. While you want to enjoy what you are doing, you always want to remember that it is a serious business.

There are some types of investing that are easier to handle as a side career or on the weekends. If this is the type of investing you are looking for, you will not want to look at day trading. This type of investing is meant to be a daily business, and many people look at it as their day job. This means that once you decide to become a day trader officially, you need to treat it as you would any other career. You must get up in the morning, get ready for your day, and make sure you are ready to work by your set time, which could be as early as 7 in the morning.

While you will have some flexibility in your schedule from a regular job, meaning you could set a bit of a later start time in the morning, you will want to make sure to set a schedule you will follow at least Monday through Friday. Even working from home, you will want to make sure to limit distractions. For example, you will not want to focus on day trading and watching television at the same time. Set up an office for yourself and pay attention to your work. Get ready for your job as a day trader like you would for your job at any other office. Do not head into your office, in your pajamas. You are more likely to feel like you want to put in 100% effort and succeed if you treat this as a career.

Day Trader Is Harder than It Looks

Day trading will not help you get rich quickly. You should not look at day trading as a get rich quick arrangement. It just means that you will probably need to spend more time learning about day trading than you initially thought. You want to make sure you are well-versed in the field before you make your first investment. I want to give you a comprehensive beginner's guide so you can learn as much as you can about day trading to start your journey in one location. In other words, I have done most of the research for you.

Trading is Different from Investing

One of the biggest rules that you should understand before becoming a day trader is this is different from investing. To help you understand the difference, here are a few basic differences between trading and investing:

As an investor, you need to have an idea where the stocks are heading in the future. However, as a day trader, you only need to concern yourself with which stocks will give you the best financial gain on that day. You look more closely at the minutes. You will not even pay much attention to the hours and will not worry about the next day, week, month, or year.

You Will Not Win Every Trade

It does not matter how experienced you become as a day trader, and there will still be days that you lose on a trade. Many people create an image in their minds where they will become so experienced at trading that they will never make a mistake, and they will only gain capital.

Every game has its rules and regulations, and day trading is not any different. In case you are new to the game, you must bear in mind the entire standard rules that have been put in place to control the game.

There are many rules of day trading that you have to familiarize yourself with irrespective of whether you specialize in forex, stocks, options, cryptocurrency, or futures. If you fail to abide by some of the rules, it can result in significant losses.

In as much as some rules differ depending on where you are located as well as the size of your trade, we will focus on the most important rules. In addition, it will equally discuss the rules that novices can put into practice as they venture into the complicated field of day trading. These rules will also aid the experienced traders to improve their performance in trade, for instance, in the area of risk management.

Get In, Exit and Escape

One major mistake that beginners make is jumping into the arena without a well thought out game plan. Do not dare to press the "enter" button if you do not have a plan of how to get in and exit. Understandably, some elements of excitement can set in when you are new in the field. However, it is important to note that if you do not have a formidable plan, you will be thrown out of the game completely. Make use of the rules of risk management as well as stop-losses cut down losses.

Timing

I bet you usually wake up early and bright, ready to face the day ahead in the day trading arena. However, avoiding the first quarter-hour when the market is opened is arguably one of the most crucial trading rules to abide by. Most of the activity that takes place at this time involves market orders or panic trades from the previous night. You should instead use this period to follow up on reversals. The most experienced day traders also avoid the first quarter-hour.

Be Conscious of Margin

Do you remember the days when you started, and you were looking for capital? It was very easy to fall for a margin. However, you should keep in mind that it is a loan. A loan that needs to be repaid in as much as it can greatly revamp your profits, it also can leave you nursing significant losses. Therefore, it is advisable to learn how to trade accordingly before resorting to the margin.

Demo Accounts

You have a lot to learn and absolutely nothing to lose by taking the initiative to first practice using a demo account. You can nurture your craft with a lot of time and space for trial and error because you are being funded by money that has been simulated.

Very many brokers will give you free accounts so that you can practice because they are the best place to learn about strategies, patterns, and charts, as well as the quarter-hour day trading practice.

Learn to Accept the Loss

Virtually all the veteran traders have all achieved what they have achieved because they were willing to lose and learn from it. Losing is just the pathway to get more experience, embrace it.

Take in Everything

One veteran once said that a great trader is similar to an athlete, he might possess, but he has to train himself on how to use them. Complacency should not be something that great traders relate to because they should always be; I am searching for that edge. This means that they resort to a wide range of resources to boost their knowledge. They can use anything, ranging from videos, books, blogs, and forums.

Do an Evaluation of Tips

It is normal to get excited when you are given a tip that is thought-provoking. Nonetheless, unconfirmed tips from relatively undependable sources can result in significant losses. Jesse Livermore, a trader, said that experience had taught him a tip or some tips that will make him more money than what his judgment can. Therefore, ensure that you double-check any information that may affect your decisions as a trader.

Rules of Risk Management

The rules of money management and the risks of day trading are key determinants of how prosperous a trader will be. In as much as you do not have to follow these rules to the letter, they have proven to be indispensable to many.

1% Risk Rule

Here, the idea is to bar you from trading beyond your ability. When you put this technique into use irrespective of whether a trade subsidy or not, you will always have some reserve I am stacked in the bank to help you correct your balance later on.

The idea is that you should never engage in trade with more than 1% of your total account on one trade. For example, if your account has $50,000, you will only use up to $500 on your trade.

Why Use It?

You will have to lose over 100 trades simultaneously to clear your bank account balance completely. This is important to safeguard your earnings when market conditions are volatile as you get good returns in the process.

I bet you are worried that you will not be raking in maximum profits if you trade so meagerly. Calm down. You can make good profits. If you stake 1%, you should expect a profit of about 1.5%—2%. If you trade several times a day, the profits will definitely make themselves evident.

It is arguably the best approach for the people that are starting. In as much as you get to experience through trial and error, losses can come fast and thick. However, if you are consistent, it will teach you the tricks of the game until you become a veteran in trading with an arsenal of techniques for making maximum profits in daily training.

Variations

As soon as you have created an efficient technique, you can make changes to your risk tolerance. You can upgrade it to 1.5% or 2%. However, it is important to note that traders with $100,000 in their accounts should not risk more than 1% in one trade because even a 1% loss could have a massive impact. It is about finding an area that you and comfortable with, and it also connects with your style of trade.

Taxes - Regional differences

Rules of income tax will vary greatly depending on where you are located, as well. To some extent, technology allows you to go beyond the confines of your city of the nation's border. However, there is usually no way of avoiding taxes. Every country will ask you to pay taxes irrespective box whether you bear in Africa, Europe, or Asia.

Chapter 25. Can I Make Profits Day Trading?

Make Money with Day Trading

Before you start trading, look around the market and make your plan on which combination of currencies you will trade. This depends on the volatility of their exchange prices, which is based on research done on the past profitable exchanges. Planning also includes the time that you are willing to sit down and monitor the trades, make sure that you stick to the time scheduled to avoid messing up the already earned profit. Remember that choosing the time to trade should be at a time when the market is more active. The market will be there tomorrow and, therefore, when your scheduled time closes your trades. Strategy to be used throughout the time you are trading should also be thought out before you start trading, and it should be adhered to throughout the trading period in the day.

When day trading, you have to know how to manage your money because at the end of the day you want to have money, not lose money. During the day, you will take part in several trades, and therefore you need to know the amount of money you will use to invest. You have to prepare for losses and gains, but the total loss you expect is of importance to avoid losing all your money at the end of the day. It starts by knowing the risk per trade; this is the amount of money you are ready to lose on one trade. The size of the account should also be taken into account. If you have a trade that, according to you, has a stop-loss of close to 50 pips, if you risk $200, your risk will be $4. It is done by dividing the amount of money you are risking by the stop loss pips.

Always have a stop target before you start trading, and also consider the type of market you are trading in; some markets are so dynamic such that your stop order might not be executed as per the set value. Therefore, to be safe, set your stops using the actual price-action and the conditions prevailing in the market. It is good to set them around the resistance, and support levels, chart patterns, trend lines, and how volatile the currencies you are using are in the market. It is not only the stop loss position that you should consider during day trading, but also consider the point at which you want to take profits. For maximum profit, place appropriate levels of making a profit.

Besides, you should look at the reward-risk ratio, and when it is 1:1, it means that the amount you are risking equal to what you expect as a profit, and 3:1 has a triple amount to gain to lose. You can mix these such trades such that you have many with a high potential of gaining and few with an equal potential of winning.

Although trading takes place at all times in the world, each market region has its hours of trade. Therefore, as a trader, you should know your market, and its opening and closing hours. You should also know that trading is not good throughout a trading day, and trading is good when the market activity is high. We have four major trading markets, and each of them has its opening and closing hours. However, some markets open around the same time.

For example, the Tokyo market opens at 7 P.M and close at 4 A.M. In comparison, the Sydney market opens at 5 P.M until 2 A.M looking at the opening hours of the two markets, there is a time when they are all open. Therefore, the level of activity with the currencies increases in the two markets between 5 P.M and 8 P.M when you are in the two markets, it is the best time to trade. It means that when more than one market is open at the same time, the trading activities are heightened, and the price of currencies fluctuates more. Therefore, maximize this by making trades when the market is very active.

You should also be alert on any news release that can make the price of the currency to fluctuate as you look out for changes in prices. Remember that the news can go against the predicted trend, and if you had already taken a position, you can either loss or gain, and it happens in seconds. You can make money by reacting correctly and within the correct time in day trading. The news to look out for is the GDP data, trade deficits, central bank meetings and announcements, consumer confidence, among other big news affecting the economy in the region.

As you look out for the fluctuations in prices, stay in check not to open so many trades that you cannot control. Having many trades does not mean that you will get a lot of money. The best thing to do is to start your trade-in small portions. Identify three trades that show potential and monitor the trends; it is good to deal with two trades in a day that you will maximize on their profits than dealing with many that you will not make money on.

The amount of money made in the day also depends on the type of trading strategy used. To make more money choose a trading system that will give you more. When using scalping, it can help you to gain more, but you should increase the number of trades because the income obtained from one trade is very small.

This is done when your main strategy is scalping. You can make more than one hundred trades in a day so that at the end of the day you have many wins than losses thus at the end of the day you have good money in your wallet.

If you are doing scalping as a supplementary strategy, you should use it when the market is not giving a large range in terms of the fluctuation of prices of currencies. In this case, most of the time, there are no trends in a longer time frame, and therefore using scalping in the short time frame becomes the best option to exploit. This way, you are assured that even without visible trends, there is a possibility that you will not end the day without money. This means that you initiate a long time frame trade, and as it develops, you start new sets of trade with a shorter time frame; it should be done in the same direction. You will then be entering and leaving the trade, as you collect small amounts, then later get a major profit with the long-time frame.

In a day, you can also use the false breakouts to make money in day trading. Looking at a trend, you can spot a breakout that you believe that it will not maintain the same direction. This is when you make a move, when the trend comes back to its original line; using this quick realization, you can make some cash. Using a fading breakout is the most effective because breakout tends to come out and out, and eventually, they succeed, but with a fading breakout, you will be sure of making money.

The rationale of using breakouts is that the resistance and support levels are known as ceilings and price floors, respectively. When one of them is broken, traders expect the trend to continue in that direction and therefore, the traders react in the opposite direction, which later stabilizes the trend to its original flow. An example is that when the resistance level is broken, most traders think that the price will continue in the upward trend and buy the currency instead of selling. You should, therefore, sell the currency, acting contrary to what everyone is doing, and when the breakout returns to normal, you buy again at a lower price.

Similarly, when the support is broken, it means that the movement of the price is downwards, and most traders are likely to sell and not buy. To collect funds from this move, you should buy the currency instead of selling, and when the price resumes to its trend line, you sell it out. This type of trading is much profitable, but it can be very risky, therefore, analyze the graph well to make sure that it is a false breakdown before you enter the trade. However, to be safer, place a limit order when buying and selling, and make sure that at the end of the day, you have money in your wallet.

You can also make money using pivot points, which helps you to determine how prices of currencies are moving. Most of the time, the pivot points will identify prices as bullish or bearish, then represent the averages for the low, high prices and closing prices occurring on a trading day. Do you need to know the market trend? The pivot points will help you with that. Use the pivot points to determine the general direction of the trade; if the market price of the currency is above the base of the pivot point, it suggests that the trade is bullish, and when it is below the pivot base, then it is bearish. Also, when using pivot points, close all the long position trades when the market gets to the resistance levels and close the short ones when the market goes below the support level.

There is also the use of a reversal strategy that is commonly used around the globe; this strategy will help you to make money within a very short time, especially if the currency is moderately volatile. To use this strategy, you will have to study the graph to determine whether it has several consecutive highs and lows. At the highest point, which is called the top, you can easily predict that the price of the currency will reverse, and then react immediately by selling the currency. Similarly, if the graph of the currency has the lowest point, which is known as the bottoms, you predict that the trend will reverse, and buy the currency. When using this strategy, as long as you have predicted the reversal of the trend correctly, you will add money to your wallet.

In day trading, you are required to enter into many trades and exiting, depending on the type of strategy you are using. Therefore, to ensure that you have your funds available for trade when you need it, make sure that you focus on more liquid currencies. Remember that liquidity also comes with volatility. If you tie your money, you will get an opportunity and fail to utilize it because you have no funds at your disposal. Alternatively, always plan your trades such that your wallet does not get depleted because trading that is triggered by a news release is not planned. Still, when it arises, it is good to take advantage of the opportunity and to make quick money or take a position that will earn you more.

Conclusion

The important thing is you take the time and effort to pay attention to the stock market and the trends of different stocks. Keep track of what you do and do things carefully. Trading shouldn't be taken lightly if you want to make money. While it can be a great way to increase your finances by the millions, it's also a great way to send you into the negative if taken lightly.

Take everything you have learned about day trading to heart, and then do what works best for you. You don't have to follow all the rules to be a success, but you do need to follow some. What works for one trader might not work for another.

The truth is that you can be making some serious cash flow within months if done correctly. Also, you need to make sure that whatever it is that you are doing is done with perfect calculations and at your own risk. We can't stress enough how calculated you have to be with your investments, as it will only lead you to make more money. Finally, make sure that you not only take care of the investments by keeping track of it but also that you ease into every investment that you earn as it will only lead you to make some smart decisions in the long run.

For those who want to take an active role in their investment activities, trading is one option to consider. It's not the same as traditional investing. Trading is aimed at earning profits over the short term. Therefore, it's more like a business than investing. Depending on the level of commitment you can give to trading, the amount of money you can risk, and your risk tolerance, you can choose a trading style that is the best fit for your situation.

Remember that trading is risky. You should never risk more capital in trading than you can afford to lose. By taking some reasonable steps, however, you can protect yourself and your capital from catastrophic losses. Don't get fooled by early losses. Beginning traders can expect to have some losses and make mistakes along the way. That's inevitable when taking up any new occupation. As long as you are not risking huge amounts of money on one single trade, you should be able to dust yourself off and get up and try again.

Some people will find it to be too much to deal with, but I hope that you will learn from your failures and do better next time, and build yourself into a successful trader with time. Remember that the most important thing for your success is the combination of your win rate and the average win rate. Too many traders focus only on the win rate and not on the latter, and the result is a very warped view of what trading is all about. Always keep your risk per trade at a manageable level with the risk of ruin zero. If possible, fix your risk per trade a few levels below the threshold to account for different mistakes you might make. Follow the simulation, demo, and live framework to implement anything with regards to your trading. Focus yourself and enjoy the process!